Dieter Neubert, Christine Scherer (eds.)

Agency and Changing World Views in Africa

Beiträge zur Afrikaforschung

ISSN 0938–7285

Herausgegeben vom Institut für Afrikastudien

in Verbindung mit dem
Kulturwissenschaftlichen Forschungskolleg SFB/FK 560
„Lokales Handeln in Afrika im Kontext globaler Einflüsse"
der Universität Bayreuth

Band

40

LIT

Agency and Changing World Views in Africa

edited by

Dieter Neubert and Christine Scherer

LIT

Gedruckt mit Unterstützung
der Deutschen Forschungsgemeinschaft, DFG.

Bibliographic information published by the Deutsche Nationalbibliothek
The Deutsche Nationalbibliothek lists this publication in the Deutsche Nationalbibliografie; detailed bibliographic data are available in the Internet at http://dnb.d-nb.de.

ISBN 978-3-643-90236-8

A catalogue record for this book is available from the British Library

Klosbachstr. 107
CH-8032 Zürich
Tel. +41 (0) 44-251 75 05
Fax +41 (0) 44-251 75 06
E-Mail: zuerich@lit-verlag.ch
http://www.lit-verlag.ch

LIT VERLAG Dr. W. Hopf
Berlin 2014
Fresnostr. 2
D-48159 Münster
Tel. +49 (0) 2 51-62 03 20
Fax +49 (0) 2 51-23 19 72
E-Mail: lit@lit-verlag.de
http://www.lit-verlag.de

Distribution:
In the UK: Global Book Marketing, e-mail: mo@centralbooks.com
In North America: International Specialized Book Services, e-mail: orders@isbs.com
In Germany: LIT Verlag Fresnostr. 2, D-48159 Münster
Tel. +49 (0) 2 51-620 32 22, Fax +49 (0) 2 51-922 60 99, E-mail: vertrieb@lit-verlag.de
In Austria: Medienlogistik Pichler-ÖBZ, e-mail: mlo@medien-logistik.at
e-books are available at www.litwebshop.de

Dedicated to the memory of Patrick Chabal

Contents

Agency and World Views: An Introduction

Dieter Neubert and Christine Scherer[1]

When the concept of globalisation gained attention in African studies in the 1990s one prominent feature of the globalisation debate was the idea of a world-wide process of economic, political, social and cultural homogenisation, the latter represented by the metaphor of McDonaldization (Ritzer 1993, 2009). This debate offered several good arguments in particular with reference to economic and political processes. The economic power of the capitalist world system was and is obviously a fact and capitalist thought was thoroughly supported by the policy of structural adjustment pursuit of the International Monetary Fund (IMF) and the World Bank. The third wave of democratisation (Huntington 1993) reached Africa after 1989 and triggered an intensive discussion on democracy in Africa, which challenged the autocratic leaders with social movements claiming democracy. Despite these processes, the homogenisation thesis could hardly convince specialists on Africa. The effects of "globalisation" were neither entirely new nor that simple to describe. The influences of alien political and economic powers are part and parcel of African history. But despite all the changes African societies underwent since the beginning of colonisation, they are far from copies of their former colonial powers.

Objections to the simple homogenisation thesis could well be supported by the numerous micro studies on local reactions towards development projects and global influences that gained momentum outside of social anthropology after the failure of the grand development theories (Neubert 2003). These studies showed and continue to demonstrate that outside influences are hardly ever simply adopted. They are either changed or appropriated by practical action to make use of these influences according to the specific needs, interests and visions. Globalisation theorists like Robertson or Appadurai gained prominence in African studies as a result. Robertson not only described globalisation as an ongoing process that began several hundred years ago, but also highlighted the

[1] We are grateful to Elísio Macamo who participated in the development of the concept of the conference, which was the starting point for this edited volume. His ideas are part of this introduction. However, any errors or shortcomings are the responsibility of the authors.

constant interaction between the global and the local, which he conceptualized in the term "glocalization" (Robertson 1992, 1998). Appadurai (1996) reminded us to look at flows between the different scapes – ethno, ideo, finance, media and technoscapes – and not focus solely on the extension of Western culture. Together with micro studies from anthropology and sociology these concepts opened the floor for the idea that processes of globalisation can only be researched empirically and understood when agency is taken into account on a local level.

The concept of agency was used to describe this active involvement of people in a local setting, i.e. agents, with the influences and processes triggered by it. The rise of the globalisation debate in African studies was therefore accompanied by the debate of agency in Africa. This specific perspective was expressed by the creation of two larger research enterprises. One of these was the research programme on "Agency in Africa: Understanding Socio-Cultural Transformations in Time and Space (2002-2006)".[2] Another large research enterprise was the Humanities' Collaborative Research Centre on "Agency in Africa in the Context of Global Influences" at the University of Bayreuth (SFB-FK 560, 2000-2007) funded by the German Research Foundation (Deutsche Forschungsgemeinschaft, DFG).

Agency was not a new concept in African studies. The Manchester School of Social Anthropology already referred to the nexus of action and structure (van Binsbergen 2007). Their studies on African urbanisation, especially in Central, East and South Africa, showed that Africans were neither caught in their traditions nor helpless victims of "de-tribalization" in the new cities. They described the active processes of social reorganisation in the cities and the appropriation not only of capitalist economies or new political institutions but also of cultural elements of the colonial powers (e.g. Mitchell 1958). Their studies focused on these active processes of social action without using the term "agency".

A much later source for the agency debate was Norman Long's adaptation of constructivist actor theories (Long 1989, 2001). He used this approach for a critical analysis of development projects and programmes and showed that

[2] The two following research programmes at the African Studies Centre in Leiden "Connections and Transformations" (2007-2011) and "Africa and Global Restructuring" (since 2012) refer at least partly to questions of agency.

many of the so-called problems and failures of development enterprises could be easily understood when seen from the perspective of the local people at whom these activities were directed (Elwert & Bierschenk 1988). One important point of Long's analysis is that agency in a local setting is of course done consciously. People skilfully pursue their interests, which frequently was and still is completely misunderstood by development agencies. Like the older Manchester School, Long and his followers highlighted the fact that Africans were and certainly are active designers of their own lives and well able to resist outside influences that were seen as destructive to their way of living. It was James Scott (1990) whose studies on South East Asia influenced this line of thought. His general understanding of agency as active social action stood in opposition to the victimizing of Africans by well-meaning patrons and underlined their capability to speak and act on their own behalf. This notion opened the door to criticism of the simplification of the homogenisation thesis in the globalisation debate. In this understanding, agency underlines the ability to act and function as a counterweight against victimisation of the so-called "helpless" African people.

Norman Long links his understanding of agency in the introduction of his sociology of development (Long 2001) to a constructivist concept, yet the largest part of the agency debate was not so much interested in the concept as such but in the description and analysis of practical local action/local practices. Here, agency basically refers to social action, in the sense of Max Weber, as directed and intentional, meaningful social action. This has to be distinguished from mere reaction or reflex action without intention or meaning like a spontaneous move of the arm to protect oneself from a falling object. We should be careful not to confuse this understanding of meaningful social action, i.e. action to which we attach meaning, with the Parsonian understanding of social action as normatively constrained. The Parsonian understanding of social action refers mainly to the guiding power of norms and highlights the binding strength of social structure. The term agency marks a different understanding of social action: one that is open for decisions and the actors' influence on social action and change, quite in line with Max Weber's original concept.[3] This concept of agen-

[3] Weber gives the example of two people riding a bicycle. An accidental crash cannot be classified as social action. The attempt to avoid a crash or a debate after a crash would be social action (Weber 1972, 10; Wirtschaft und Gesellschaft § 1. II.3).

cy underlines the distance to the Parsonian concept of social action and highlights the active participation and the leeway for social actors in social action (see Goetze in this volume for a discussion of the agency concept).

For Weber the capability for intentional, meaningful social action is inherent in every human being. However, in parts of the agency debate, the term agency became a characteristic of particular strong persons or groups. Several studies tried to emphasize that these people *have* agency and readers should be reminded that the victimisation of humans, i.e. Africans, ignores their active and purposeful engagement with their environment. This conclusion is certainly right, but less surprising than it is naive (van Dijk, Bruijn and Gewald 2007: 6). Other studies focus on the strength and power of African social movements to appropriate the consequences of globalisation on their own terms (van Binsbergen & van Dijk 2004). As van Binsbergen and van Dijk (2004: 42f) put it, this presents "[…] African actors as conscious and creative strategic actors whose remaining choice, despite the constraints of objective globalizing conditions, is still considerable." This understanding of agency emphasizes "human creativity and resilience" (van Dijk, de Bruijn and Gewald 2007: 1; see also Probst & Spittler 2004), or the capability of "improvisation" as Dorsch shows in this volume. It furthermore emphasizes the element of reflexivity (van Dijk, de Bruijn and Gewald 2007: 8), which is reminiscent of Max Weber's intentional and meaningful social action. In other studies agency was directly connected to emancipatory concepts and visions or as a norm for successful social action. This turned the openness of agency upside down. Patrick Chabal's analysis in this volume criticizes in particular this hostage-taking of the concept of agency by political emancipatory activists.

Any normative exaggeration of agency is not helpful for a sound analysis, but it is also not easy to provide a general and widely-accepted definition of agency. As Emirbayer and Mische show in their article "What is Agency?" (1998), nearly all social theories have a specific concept of agency. However, Emirbayer's and Mische's definition covers quite well the core elements of the basic understanding of agency in African studies:

> "We define it [human agency] as the temporally constructed engagement by actors of different structural environments – the temporal-relational contexts of action – which, through the interplay of habit, imagination, and judgment, both reproduces and transforms those structures in interactive

> response to the problems posed by changing historical situations. This definition encompasses what we shall analytically distinguish below as the different constitutive elements of human agency: iteration, projectivity, and practical evaluation" (Emirbayer & Mische 1998: 970).

Emirbayer and Mische put agency in a timeframe and their three constitutive elements mark dimensions that refer to the past (iteration as being influenced by traditions and habits created in the past), to the future (projectivity as the ability to think and plan alternative futures) and to the present (practical evaluation as the necessity to bring past experiences and visions of the future together with the possibility to learn from the past).

At first sight, this definition of agency seems to include rational choice concepts commonly used in positivist sociology and economy (Goldthorpe 1998, March 1978, Simon 1955). But Emirbayer and Mische see an important difference. From their perspective rational choice theory does not fully manage to consider the embeddedness in specific contexts into their concept (Emirbayer & Mische 1998: 966f). Especially the need for contextualisation highlighted in Emirbayer's and Mische's article has been one of the core points of the agency debate on Africa since its beginning. The Manchester School and its followers in social anthropology and the development debate influenced by Norman Long's approach highlight the specific emic perspectives or the perspective of the actors by contextualisation.

Agency approaches at least implicitly assume that the actors act in their social and cultural context as postulated by structural functionalism from Malinowski to Parsons. This context is represented by tradition and habits that affect iteration; however, traditions and habits do not bind or even pre-empt the social action. For the theoretical debate it is of greatest importance to analyse how the interplay unwinds between given norms and habits that represent the context on the one hand, and the deliberate decision making or practical evaluation and the possibility to think and create another future in the sense of projectivity on the other.[4]

For our analysis of agency in Africa it is more important to understand and conceptualize what has been called the "context" in the process of defining

---

4 This has been discussed systematically in the mentioned article by Emirbayer and Mische (1998). It contributes to the discussion on social theory in general and its core question concerning the relation between agency (social action) and structure.

agency. The theoretical question is how the embeddedness into sociocultural conditions with specific world views can be captured, how the embeddedness translates into a view of agency and how this embeddedness in turn changes as a result of interaction. This interplay between agency and concepts of the world is the core focus of this book.

The question of context becomes essential because the encounters triggered by globalisation (some would prefer to talk of modernity, see Macamo & Neubert in this volume) between local people and, generally speaking, outside influences are not only encounters between different institutions or individuals but often between different ways of understanding and conceptualizing the world.

The metaphor of the "battlefields of knowledge" (Long & Long 1992) expresses this encounter in the terminology of the sociology of knowledge. Another conceptualisation in line with Berger and Luckmann's (1966) and Erving Goffman's (1980) constructivism is the term "frame of reference", as we stated elsewhere:

> "By this we mean the standards of evaluation and orientation which can be applied by actors in a specific situation and which make fundamental statements about the actual and ideal nature of the world. Reality is interpreted with the help of and within central frames of reference. This interpretation offers an essential basis for individual decisions to act, independently of the situative requirements. Frames of reference are thus a form of supraindividual orientation and they apply to groups of people" (Loimeier, Neubert and Weißköppel 2005: 12).

The links to the Emirbayer and Mische definition are obvious. Frames of reference provide the criteria for individual acts of decision and mediate in Emirbayer and Mische's terms between iteration and practical evaluation. At least indirectly, frames of reference are the background for projectivity. This conceptualisation of the context for social action is already operationalized and linked to a specific theoretical approach. But it would restrict the contributors of this book to this particular understanding of constructivism. The term "world view" in the sense of the German term "Weltanschauung" is more open and does not pre-empt a defined way of operationalisation. Our understanding of the term "Weltanschauung" is closely related to the work of Husserl (e.g. 1996) and thus reflects the general orientation towards constructivism of the contributors to this volume. According to Knies (2011: 39), for Husserl, "Weltanschauung" refers to a limited understanding of the world, relative to the particular traditions of experience and praxis in which it takes shape and functions. In other words "world view" can be understood as a set of perspectives of the world that weigh on action and interpretive frameworks on the nature of reality. These frameworks are produced by actors, but also provide contexts themselves within which agency unfolds. The same world is thus described, understood and analysed differently from the perspective of different world views. This difference is emphasized by the concept of world views we are applying here.

Examples of such world views (or interpretive frameworks) can be drawn from religious, economic, political, social and scientific notions about the nature of reality. In the context of globalisation these notions are expressed in human rights, concepts of law, democracy, specific, political philosophies or neoliberalism for instance, all of which may claim an interpretive hegemony as Macamo and Neubert show in this volume.

All so-called "world religions" provide excellent examples of world views and their expansion across the globe, and underline the fact that globalisation has a considerable historical dimension. These world views are not static; they undergo change and inhere in social processes in local contexts. Individuals in such contexts engage with these world views and, in the process, relations of power may prove decisive for outcomes such as rejection, appropriation and hybridisation or, less frequently, indifference or a vibrant negotiation between different "world views" and "frames of references".

The analysis of different reactions to the encounters of local agency with outside influences in the context of globalisation has been a core objective of the collaborative research centre and its publications. The first collective book "Between Resistance and Expansion" (Probst & Spittler 2004) focusses in part on resistance towards the harmonisation in a world culture in the sense of McDonaldization[5]. It also shows multiple ways of making use of ideas, goods and institutions on local terms through appropriation. The question of syncretisation or hybridisation in the sense of creative compositions of local and global elements as the creation of something new is the main theme of the second edit-

---

[5] This should not be confused with the world society approach of Meyer et al. Meyer et al. postulate the existence of a single world culture though with their notion of de-coupling and recognize the fact that homogenisation is often superficial (Meyer et al.1997).

ed book "Unpacking the New. Rethinking Cultural Syncretisation in Africa and Beyond" (Adogame, Echtler and Vierke 2008). While these two perspectives focus on a particular relation between local agency and global influences such as resistance to global influences or syncretisation, the third perspective presented in this volume follows a different path. The analysis is not centred on a specific relation between local agency and global influences but rather on a particular form of influences: world views. We will focus on the interplay between "outside" and "inside" influences and how the local population handles these processes, and also discuss the possible changes of world views once they have travelled from one culture to another. The works on travelling models (Czarniawska & Sevón 2005; Czarniawska & Joerges 1996; Rottenburg 1996) remain in our interest. This approach starts from a neo-institutionalist perspective and highlights the fact that the models are themsleves subject to change in the processes of trans-lation. It follows the journey of one particular model through different worlds and analyses its changes, whereas in this volume we are interested in situations in which different models are confronted with each other and how the actors mediate between the two. This naturally includes the possibility that a model may be translated into and appropriated in the local context.

This book now brings together two directions of thought: it includes contributions that pursue a theoretical objective and conceptualize or discuss agency on the one hand, and world views based on different theoretical approaches on the other. The contributions of Macamo & Neubert and Goetze focus each on a theoretical debate, while Patrick Chabal examines the concept of agency itself and reveals its normative implications in much of the contemporary thinking on Africa. In sketching how Africa indeed domesticates modernity Chabal clearly points out that distinct scholarly implications of agency carry some obvious analytical risks linked to diametral poles of understanding "Agency in Africa". Dieter Goetze refers to the sociological background of the relation between agency and world views, but he scrutinizes the impact of "world views of globalisation". Their refence to a single actor and to market integration creates specific conditions of agency which he conceptualizes using a social mechanism approach. The first three articles put the revision of agency as an encompassing concept into perspective to provide a critical understanding of the ambiguities involved, while van Beek develops his theoretical reflections on an in-depth empirical study of the Kapsiki of North Cameroon and their understanding of how and why things go wrong. He points out that agency is too often conceptualized as a solely positive (re)action to external influences and neglects the destructive and harmful agency that "happens" in the immediate environment.

Most of the contributions in this volume focus on the tensions between world views claiming global validity and world views that claim local validity. Therefore, the second group of articles in this book looks at the confrontation of world views in particular cases and discusses these on distinct empirical grounds. The contributions of Oberauer, Sippel & Wanitzek and Howell focus on conflicting concepts of law and the corresponding juridical norms. Oberauer's contribution on the Islamic institution of Waqf under colonial domination in Zanzibar examines the tensions between two interacting law systems – British and Islamic law – which each represent a world view claiming universal applicability. Howell offers an understanding of both the North-South relationship in the contested context of international "Intercountry Adoption" in which countries of the South try to assert their national legal position against the North: The UN Convention on the Rights of the Child and the Hague Con-vention. Nevertheless, the agency of both parties in the conflict is based on and informed by corresponding juridical norms. Similarly, the chapter by Sippel and Wanitzek describes, with reference to the empirical grounds exemplified by means of a village in Tanzania, how the encompassing programme "law and development" for developing and transition countries can be conceptualized as a special case of changing world views. The deep impact of a legal pluralism in the local arena and the ignorance against local mechanisms of finding solutions becomes traceable here. In contrast, Dorsch points to the hidden effects on individuals in dealing with distinct world views at once. In his chapter he presents a case study on Mozambiquans who went to Cuba for education and studies and shows that the agents are not confronted with a simple local-global dichotomy, but with a complex interplay of at least two competing frames of reference within a global scope: socialist internationalism vs. neo-liberal globalisation.

To conclude, the third volume once again offers an empirically embedded qualitative discussion on "Local Agency in Africa in the Context of Global Influences". This time agency is related to views of the world that offer powerful frames of reference. The impacts these have come along with the actors on the ground who confront and choose, reconcile and negotiate, shape or just explain and sometimes also accept the "worlds" and "views" in their constant change.

References

Adogame, Afe, Magnus Echtler, and Ulf Vierke (eds.) (2008): *Unpacking the New. Rethinking Cultural Syncretization in Africa and Beyond.* Münster, Hamburg, Berlin: Lit.

Appadurai, Arjun (1996): *Modernity at Large.* Minneapolis: University of Minnesota Press.

Berger, Peter and Thomas Luckmann (1980): *Die gesellschaftliche Konstruktion der Wirklichkeit.* Frankfurt: Fischer.

Binsbergen, Wim van (2007): Manchester as the Birth Place of Modern Agency Research: The Manchester School Explained from the Perspective of Evans-Pritchard's Book "The Nuer". In: Mirjam de Bruijn, Rijk van Dijk and Jan-Bart Gewald (eds.): *Strength beyond Structure. Social and Historical Trajectories of Agency in Africa.* Leiden: Brill, 16-61.

Binsbergen, Wim van, Rijk van Dijk and Jan-Bart Gewald (2004): *Situating Globality: African Agency in the Appropriation of Global Culture.* Leiden, Boston: Brill.

Binsbergen, Wim van, Rijk van Dijk and Jan-Bart Gewald (2004): Situating Globality: African Agency in the Appropriation of Global Culture: An Introduction. In: Wim van Binsbergen, Rijk van Dijk and Jan-Bart Gewald (eds.): *Situating Globality: African Agency in the Appropriation of Global Culture.* Leiden, Boston: Brill, 3-54.

Bruijn, Mirjam de, Rijk van Dijk and Jan-Bart Gewald, (eds.) (2007): *Strength beyond Structure. Social and Historical Trajectories of Agency in Africa.* Leiden: Brill.

Czarniawska, Barbara and Bernward Joerges (1996): Travel of Ideas. In: Barbara Czarniawska and Guje Sevón (eds.): *Translating Organizational Change.* Berlin, New York, 12-48.

Czarniawska, Barbara and Guje Sevón (eds.) (2005): *Global Ideas. How Ideas, Objects and Practices Travel in the Global Economy.* Copenhagen: Liber & Copenhagen Business School Press.

Dijk, Rijk van, Mirjam de Bruijn and Jan-Bart Gewald (2007): Social and Historical Trajectories of Agency in Africa: An Introduction. In: Mirjam de Bruijn, Rijk van Dijk and Jan-Bart Gewald (eds.) : *Strength beyond Structure. Social and Historical Trajectories of Agency in Africa.* Leiden: Brill, 1-15.

Elwert, Georg and Thomas Bierschenk (1988): Development Aid as an Intervention in Dynamic Systems: An Introduction. *Sociologia Ruralis* 28, 2/3, 99-112.

Emirbayer, Mustafa and Ann Mische (1998): What is Agency? *American Journal of Sociology* 103(4), 962-1023.

Probst, Peter and Gerd Spittler (2004): *Explorations of Local Vitality in Africa.* Berlin, Hamburg, Münster: Lit.

Goffman, Erving (1980): *Rahmen-Analyse. Ein Versuch über die Organisation von Alltagserfahrungen.* Frankfurt/M.: Suhrkamp.

Goldthorpe, John H. (1998): Rational Action Theory for Sociology. *The British Journal of Sociology* 49/2, 167-192.

Huntington, Samuel P. (1993): *The Third Wave: Democratization in the Late Twentieth Century.* Norman et al.: University of Oklahoma Press.

Husserl, Edmund (1996): *Die Krisis der europäischen Wissenschaften und die transzendentale Phänomenologie. Eine Einleitung in die phänomenologische Philosophie.* 3rd ed. Hamburg: Felix Meiner Verlag.

Knies, Kenneth (2011): Three Views of the One True World and What They Make of Mere Worldviews: A Husserlian Approach to Weltanschauung. *Humana. Mente Journal of Philosophical Studies* 18, 39-54.

Loimeier, Roman, Dieter Neubert and Cordula Weißköppel (eds.) (2005): *Globalisierung im lokalen Kontext: Perspektiven und Konzepte von Handeln in Afrika.* Münster: Lit.

Loimeier, Roman, Dieter Neubert and Cordula Weißköppel (eds.) (2005): Globalization in the Local Context. Perspectives and Concepts of Action in Africa. An Introduction. *Bayreuth African Studies Online* 2. Bayreuth: Institut für Afrikastudien & Kulturwissenschaftliches Forschungskolleg (SFB/FK 560).

Long, Norman (ed.) (1989): *Encounters at the Interface. A Perspective on Social Discontinuities in Rural Development.* Wageningen: Agricultural University.

Long, Norman (2001): *Development Sociology. Actor Perspectives.* London. New York: Routledge.

Long, Norman and Ann Long (eds.) (1992): *The Battlefields of Knowledge: The Interlocking of Theory and Practice in Social Research and Development.* London: Routledge.

Macamo, Elìsio and Dieter Neubert (2008): The New and Its Temptations. Products of Modernity and their Impact on Social Change in Africa. In: Afe Adogame, Magnus Echtler and Ulf Vierke (eds.): *Unpacking the New. Rethinking Cultural Syncretization in Africa and Beyond.* Münster, Hamburg, Berlin: Lit, 271-303.

March, James G.(1978): Bounded Rationality, Ambiguity, and the Engineering of Choice. *The Bell Journal of Economics* 9 (2), 587-608.

Meyer, John W., John Boli, George M. Thomas and Francisco Ramirez (1997): World Society and the Nation-State. *The American Journal of Sociology* 103, 144-181.

Mitchell, J. Clyde (1958): *The Kalela Dance.* Manchester: Manchester University Press.

Neubert, Dieter (2003): Entwicklungssoziologie: empirische Wende und Ansätze zur neuen Theoriebildung. In: Barbara Orth, Thomas Schwietring and Johannes Weiß (eds.): *Soziologische Forschung: Stand und Perspektiven.* Opladen: Leske & Budrich, 111-124.

Probst, Peter and Gerd Spittler (eds.) (2004): *Between Resistance and Expansion: Explorations of Local Vitality in Africa.* Berlin, Hamburg, Münster: Lit.

Ritzer, George (1993): *The McDonaldization of Society: An Investigation into the Changing Character of Contemporary Social Life.* Thousand Oaks et al.: Pine Forge Press.

— (2009): *Enchaning a Disenchanted World: Continuity and Change in the Cathedrals of Consumption.* Thousand Oaks et al.: SAGE Publications Inc.

Robertson, Roland (1992): *Globalization: Social Theory and Global Culture.* London et al.: Sage.

— (1998): Glokalisierung: Homogenität und Heterogenität in Raum und Zeit. In: Ulrich Beck (ed.): *Perspektiven der Weltgesellschaft.* Frankfurt/M.: Suhrkamp, 192-220.

Rottenburg, Richard (1996) When Organization Travels: On Intercultural Translation. In: Barbara Czarniawska and Guje Sevón (eds.): *Translating Organizational Change*. Berlin, New York: de Gruyter, 191-240.

Scott, James C. (1990): *Domination and the Arts of Resistance. Hidden Transcripts.* New Haven, London: Yale University Press.

Simon, Herbert A.(1955): A Behavioral Model of Rational Choice. *The Quarterly Journal of Economics* 69 (1), 99-118.

Weber, Max (1972): *Wirtschaft und Gesellschaft.* Tübingen: J.C.B. Mohr.

Modernity and the Globalisation of Scientific-Technological Rationality

Elísio Macamo and Dieter Neubert

Scientific-technical rationality is one of the most important foundations of modern industrial and post-industrial countries. The material world of these societies is either subject to scientific analysis or the result of technical forms of production, or both. It is linked to a particular type of reasoning which combines development theories with empirical evidence created by laboratory experiments or gathered through systematic measurement of the phenomena under investigation. Of course, scientific-technical rationality is not the only way through which one can understand the world. Religion(s), for example, offer an alternative, albeit a completely different one. As we know from our everyday life decisions are often not based on scientific-technical theories, but rather on social convention and moral or religious beliefs. At the same time, however, it is fair to assume that an overwhelming majority of the people in industrial and post-industrial societies refer to scientific-rationality for making sense of our (material world). They hardly acknowledge any other (rational) way of explanation[1]. On close inspection, though, it can be argued that the dominance of scientific-technical rationality is surprising because most people are not able to understand all the different theories used in the broad field of science in detail. They, or we, simply place trust on the underlying form of rationality or world view. According to our findings from our empirical research on local interpretations, prevention, and coping with disaster in Mozambique, Germany and the USA[2] it was obvious that the specific way of looking at and making sense of the world differs from one local setting to another. This leads to the question how a specific way of looking at the world and making sense of it can become relevant in a given context. We will offer, in this chapter, a conceptual framework to answer this question with reference to the globalisation of scientific-

---

1 This also holds true for "creationists" who view the origin of the world from a biblical perspective but do not doubt the validity of scientific-technical knowledge in other fields.

2 The project was part of the collaborative research programme (SFB 564) "Local Action in Africa in the Context of Global Influences" funded by the German Research Foundation (DFG).

technological rationality. From our sociological perspective we conceptualise specific ways of looking at the world and making sense of it as "frames of reference" in the sense of tools that can be deployed to make sense of the structure of social action in local settings. In so doing we will try to link conceptual ideas developed earlier[3] into a single framework. These bear on the relationship between world views or "frames of reference", as we put it here, and action. In other words, we will be concerned to show that social action is often caught between clashing world views and that the best way to understand the decisions which individuals and communities take concerning courses of action might consist in making the underlying world views explicit, especially through the ways in which they become locally relevant. Empirically our article draws from the aforementioned research project. Comparisons of these case studies, especially the case studies of Mozambique and the USA, will be useful in distilling some relevant insights to our central claim that social action in general, and coping with crises and disasters in particular, is shaped by the ways in which different world views accommodate one another in local settings.

World views in competition: science and technology versus religion and magic

Our empirical work in Mozambique focussed on the village of "Patrice Lumumba". This village was struck by a flood in the year 2000 (Christie & Hanlon 2001). Given the rural nature of the particular setting of the village and the concomitant rural social profile of its inhabitants we were struck during our fieldwork by the fact that our informants tended to account for the flood with reference to scientific ways of reasoning. These sat uneasily on the general intellectual orientation of the village, which drew heavily from forms of reasoning less encumbered by the strictures of science. In any case, informants told us that heavy rains in South Africa and the late opening of South African dams had led to exceptionally high floodwaters that came in waves, crashed over the existing dykes, inundated the plains and stayed for much longer than usual. To be sure, an account such as this one does not require any form of scientific literacy to be made. Yet, our curiosity was sharpened by the fact that this knowledge did not

3 Loimeier, Neubert and Weißköppel 2005, Macamo & Neubert 2008.

seem to have any kind of effect on what local communities did in response. The government's early warning system based on data from the whole Limpopo river system had predicted the flood and had warned the people via radio and mobile loudspeakers. At first people did not heed these warnings as they were in contradiction with the results of local ways of ascertaining the likelihood of floods. In other words, even though our informants were aware of how the local conveyer of scientific rationality, i.e. the state disaster relief agency, saw the natural processes they did not seem to take those accounts seriously enough to act upon them. In any case, they seemed to have strong reasons not to wish to respond to the acquired knowledge accordingly. As a consequence of this they were caught by surprise by the floods and paid dearly for their inconsequence.

On closer inspection, however, it became clear that local individuals and communities had indeed responded to the impending natural event. However, they had done so in ways that were consistent with local perceptions. Within the framework of the scientific-technical accounts they had offered us, the most rational way to react to floods would have been to pay more attention, in their reasoning over them, to ways of preventing them through securing better management of South African dams upstream. This would have corresponded to a concern with questions centring on "how" a natural event is possible. In other words, a "how" approach sought answers that focussed on a detailed chain of functional cause-effect relationships. Instead, it turned out that they were much more concerned with "why" the floods had taken place. In so doing they focussed their attention not so much on the failure of technology, but rather on their own failure to secure the benevolence of metaphysical forces which placed themselves beyond their control. To put it simply, "why" explanations referred to the triggers of the action of a metaphysical entity and not to how the entity itself acts (the difference between "how" and "why" question is elaborated in Macamo & Neubert in print). In the event, the "why" question yielded explanations which drew heavily from religious and ethical accounts such as lack of respect for the ancestors, too much sorcery and lack of communal harmony. Beneath the veneer of scientific-technical rationality suggested by their initial responses to our queries, it became clear that locally intelligible explanations based on metaphysical accounts were at the centre of the local discourse as members tried to understand why they had been so vulnerable to a natural occurrence that is part and parcel of their experience.

In a sense, therefore, there was a tension mediating the perception of natural hazards and the ways of coping with them. This tension boiled down to an opposition between a scientific-technical rationality and an experiential one, which, to use terminology first employed by Alonzo Plough and Sheldon Krimsky (1987: 8) in a paper discussing the emergence of risk communication studies, could be conceptualised as a tension between a technical rationality and a cultural rationality.[4] In fact, further research confirmed the strength of this hypothesis, namely the presence of such a tension. In a small comparative field study in the US Tennessee Valley, situated in the so-called "Bible Belt", we found a similar tension between scientific-technical and religious discourses. The latter sought to account for extreme natural events with reference to God and punishment for sinful life. Interestingly enough, and unlike in Patrice Lumumba village, a considerable part of the respondents on the Tennessee Valley in the USA, also gave "why" answers to our queries concerning the causes of the natural events, but focussed on the "how" in their actual action. To put it simply, prevention and corresponding activities were focussed on technical questions of dam and dyke construction or on straightening the river bed.

As we can see, in both cases we can ascertain the simultaneous presence of two completely different forms of rationality, if for the time being we can be granted this shorthand. Each suggests one course of action, but in actual fact each one of them leads to action of a different type, i.e. a type that is not consistent with the underlying form of rationality. Therefore, we need to ask, and conceptually grasp, a broad question, namely under what conditions forms of rationality determine action and, more specifically, why the scientific-technical form is more relevant in the US than in Mozambique and, conversely, why the metaphysical form is more relevant in the latter than in the former. In the remainder of this paper we will address these questions by focusing mainly on conceptual issues. For reasons to be explained later we suggest the use of the notion of "world views" in lieu of forms of rationality. Our main concern will be to discuss the factors that shape the globalisation of "world views". This is

4 The term "cultural rationality" can be potentially just as misleading as the local versus scientific knowledge opposition (Antweiler 1998) because of its implication that "scientific knowledge" is somehow separate from culture. What we argue in this article is that scientific knowledge is not only part of a specific culture, but also, and often, is present at the local level as well.

another way of claiming that the encounter between local settings and external influences takes place against the background of the spread of frames of reference across the globe. After clarifying these conceptual issues we will demonstrate their usefulness by applying them in the interpretation of our empirical material.

Frames of reference and "actants": world views and the material world

As already stated, from the perspective of sociology the general term of "world views" can be conceptualised as "frames of reference". The general theoretical and analytical assumption that we are making by using the idea of frames of reference is that social action takes place within a context that can be made explicit and, above all, without which an account of social action cannot be complete. In a word, frames of reference are "standards of evaluation and orientation which can be applied by actors in a specific situation and which make fundamental statements about the actual and ideal nature of the world. Reality is interpreted with the help of and within central frames of reference. This interpretation offers an essential basis for individual decisions to act, independently of the situational requirements. Frames of reference are thus a form of supra-individual orientation and they apply to groups of people." (Loimeier, Neubert and Weißköppel 2005: 12).

In some cases the range of application of a frame of reference can be extended far beyond its original area of application. These frames become globally known and can be globally effective. We will refer to these as "global frames of reference" (Loimeier, Neubert and Weißköppel 2005: 12-15).

"Global frames of reference" in this sense are for example:

- the "world" religions as a formalised framework for interpreting the world and justifying values,
- (natural) science as a formalised analytical framework for explaining the world,
- international law (including human rights and international commercial law) as a formalised legal framework for international cooperation (Loimeier, Neubert and Weißköppel 2005: 13)

All these frames "involve specific assumptions about the actual and ideal nature of the world, which have a great influence on the pre-structuring" of social action in everyday life (Loimeier, Neubert and Weißköppel 2005: 13). The reference to assumptions about the actual and ideal nature of the world makes clear that frames of reference in this sense do not include fashions in the field of music or clothes, nor globally accepted rules in sports (football or chess), although the aesthetic standards and performance values which these imply may warrant the claim that fashion and rules are undergirded by frames of reference akin to world views. We will not pursue these distinctions further here, as they would lead us into an interesting, but rather irrelevant discussion as far as our immediate interest here is concerned. Such a discussion might have to articulate the concepts of lifestyle, social milieu, scene and social settings in ways that go beyond the scope of our article.

The link to social action is important, too. Frames of reference may be widely known, but they only become effective when they guide social action. They achieve this in spatially relevant ways. To put it differently, frames of reference can be relevant in a local or in a trans-local setting. This is consistent with their articulation with norms, rules and assumptions about the world. It is in the nature of norms, rules and assumptions to be context-dependent for their validity and fruition. Michael Walzer develops a similar argument, albeit with reference to moral obligations. He argues for the existence of thick and thin morality by which he means that certain moral frameworks have a local bearing, whereas others have a more universal bearing (Walzer 1994). For the purposes here we would like to stress the point that frames of reference can be universally valid (global frames of reference), i.e. their scope can transcend local settings. Already mentioned examples are science and international law, which happen to pursue their claim to validity rather vigorously.[5]

Now, when we talk about agency in Africa in the context of external influences, global frames of reference are important factors to the extent that they bring external influences to local settings. At least for sociologists the use of the term "frames of reference" leads to questions whether this concept is linked to Erving Goffman who used the term "frames" as a key concept in his "frame

---

[5] Monotheistic religions make a global claim, too. However, in the politically globalised UN, world religions are more or less forced to accept other world views, whereas international law and science are less contested at this level.

analysis" (Goffman 1980). Our understanding of frames of reference shares with Goffman's "frame analysis" an epistemological background with a strong element of constructivism. However, our definition overlaps only partly with Goffman's understanding. Goffman is concerned with everyday life interaction. He is interested in the processes that make interaction between people possible and asks for elements that structure interactions. In Goffman's analytic concept all situations of everyday life have their specific frames which may be constructed in the particular situation and/or refer to longer existing frames at the same time. Only "primary frames" in Goffman's terminology resemble the overall "frames of reference" described before. However, not all of Goffman's primary frames are "frames of reference" in the strict sense of our definition.

There is a sense, therefore, in which one could be led to surmise that the topic of "world views" or "frames of reference" implies that we are mainly dealing with constructions. At first glance constructionism seems highly plausible as far as religious beliefs like Christianity and Islam or normative orientations like human rights, democracy, (neo-)liberalism or political world views like nationalism are concerned. This weakens somewhat when we change the subject and look at scientific-technological rationality. Its products like a car, a dam or a dyke, an aircraft, or an AK 47 gun are hardly mere constructions in this sense. They are material objects that are directly touchable and usable and they may also at times produce deadly effects. It is not that constructionism would claim that objects do not exist, even though more radical versions of it might suggest as much (Ernst von Glasersfeld 1995). The problem with radical constructionism is that it tends to underestimate, at times even leaves out of account the material world. Softer versions of constructionism simply lay stress on how we come to perceive the world and the objects in it. In this connection it might be useful to mention the work of John Searle, which while not being strictly constructionist in orientation does seem to offer ways of engaging with constructed realities while at the same time acknowledging the fact that there are classes of objects that do have an independent existence (Searle 1995). Whatever the case, though, if we are serious about frames of reference and world views we do need to enquire into the nature of our perception of the world and, conceptually, we may need to find ways of grasping the world both in its materiality and non-materiality.

The French sociologist Bruno Latour has suggested some interesting ways of coming to better grips with the interplay between the material world and frames, or more generally world views. Latour's work is especially interesting for our case because of his research on science and the claims it makes. In his earlier work on the pasteurisation of France (Latour 1984) he tried to deconstruct the understanding of science – read natural science – as a considerable part of the success of scientific theories was linked to its perfect semi-public staging of "experiments" and the successful construction of science **as if it were** based on facts. According to this analysis the success of scientific theories is not so much based on experiments as on public politics.[6]

In Latour's later work such as in "We Have Never Been Modern" (Latour 1993) he tries to integrate the material world in his theoretical concept of the "actor-network-theory" which he developed with others (Bellinger & Krieger 2006). This theory includes not only human but also non-human actors. This is the reason why Latour coined the term "actant" to capture the emergence of a form of agency that cannot be accounted for with reference to either humans or non-humans. Actants are concrete material entities that are strongly linked with human beings in one network. Actants shape the possibilities of agency. Take the hotel key, for instance, an example used by Latour himself to describe his idea of an actor-network theory which provides the context for the emergence of "actants". The need of hotel managers to ensure that it was not lost, and they did not lose money minting keys all the time, dictated that they were weighted, thereby acting upon hotel guests to leave them at the reception desk. A programme of action provided the immediate context within which hotel keys acquired agency alongside human actors.

Putting the pieces together we see in fact in Latour's concept a kind of a triad consisting of the material world, conceptual constructions and the development of a specific institutional framework. This triad must work together for the successful dissemination of a certain concept and of the notion of science in general. In this connection, it seems important to note that Latour criticises the concept of modernity in a fundamental way. This criticism bears strongly on the issues under discussion in this section. Starting from the premise that there is an

[6] This radical constructivist thesis has been a core topic in the so-called "science studies" or the "sociology of science" (Bonß & Hartmann 1985, Knorr-Cetina 1999, Neubert & Macamo 2005).

assumption according to which what distinguishes pre-modern and modern societies is the conflation of nature and society by the former on the one hand, and the conflation of the two by the latter, on the other hand, Latour argues that as current concerns with climate change, health epidemics and other environmental scares show the assumption that modernity achieved this distinction is not tenable. He states this claim in a radical fashion by saying that we have never been modern, by which he means that nature and society play just as central a role in modern life in the form of hybrids. In other words, as far as Latour is concerned hybrid objects are not only a part of "pre-modern" societies, but also part and parcel of contemporary modern societies as well. Hybrids are the outcome of the interaction among natural phenomena, social phenomena and discourses about the first two. Hybrids suggest a parliament of things, where the constitution of the social world cannot be reduced to human agency simply. It is in this sense that Latour would consider the concept of modernity as useless or even false. Indeed, he makes a plea for a symmetric anthropology which highlights the similarities between so-called "pre-modernity" and "modernity".

While in our own work we do seek to make the distinction between the pre-modern and the modern theoretically and analytically useful, we find it hard to follow Latour in the full breadth of his argument. His is an idiosyncratic definition of modernity which focuses on one aspect concerning the distinction between natural and social phenomena at the expense of structural and ideational features acquired by societies over the years, particularly with the advent of industrial based capitalism. In fact, it is the extensive use of technology, which is characteristic of industrial societies, that calls for an engagement with modern society. This engagement does not limit itself to ascertaining the extent to which a society has been able to distinguish natural from social phenomena. Rather, it takes the full range of options and constraints that became constitutive of society in important ways. Humans are similar, but the social arrangements by which they achieve life together are not. Understanding humans and their societies seems to require, we believe, distinctions which acknowledge such differences in these arrangements. It so happens that in the development of human societies, technology and the underlying scientific rationality that goes with it, came to play an important role, albeit to different degrees in different societies. We need to ask questions concerning how this role has played out in different societies and what aspects of the use of technology have thereby been decisive.

Bruno Latour takes his cue from, among other examples, the 18th century discussion on the possibility of creating a vacuum. "The air's spring can be verified everywhere, provided that one hooks up to an air pump that spreads little by little throughout Europe owing to the multiple transformations of the experimenters" (Latour 1993: 119). Without this institutional environment the scientific "facts" lose evidence. "[...] we might compare scientific facts to frozen fish; the cold chain that keeps them fresh must not be interrupted, however briefly" (Latour 1993: 119).[7]

The question is whether Latour's analysis, which was developed drawing from examples from Europe, can be applied to Africa and, furthermore, whether this would help us to understand the conflict between the scientific-technological and the religious-metaphysical frame of reference. There is no unequivocal answer that can be given to this question. Latour's work analyses a sui generis development which in its various manifestations was a response to a self-driven process of innovation, technological development and adoption. Technological progress, social change and the development of new institutional frameworks fuelled social and political dynamics that were specific to the particular circumstances of Enlightenment Europe. It is unlikely therefore that an analysis of Europe's experience with science and technology can yield comparative tools that can be translated one-to-one into other settings. This does not, however, defeat the purpose of making Europe's experience useful to an understanding of other settings. It is simply a reminder that concepts come into their own when they are applied in ways that are sensitive to context. In this sense, the question is not whether Latour can be applied to Africa, but rather what insights can be elicited from his analysis that can inform a discussion of the manner in which science and technology impact African society.

This is all the more so, since the situation in Africa (especially Africa South of the Sahara) is by all accounts fundamentally different. While the scientific frame of reference as well as the institutional framework in which it is embedded (schools, universities, research institutions) exists already, both found their way into Africa as "turnkey packages". They were developed, constructed and produced elsewhere and foisted upon societies which unlike Enlightenment

[7] This focus on the interaction of an institutional environment and the dissemination of a certain world view can be found in the work of other scholars, like Foucault or Scott (Scott 1998).

Europe did not have the kinds of social dynamics that seem to have shaped the emergence and adoption of science and technology in Europe. To put it differently, the African social setting lacked – and continues perhaps to lack – the class of inventors, experimenters, scientific debate as well as the generally greater uncertainty over the validity of knowledge that was typical of Europe in the seventeenth and eighteenth centuries which together were crucial in shaping the adoption of science in the very specific ways that came to be typical of Europe. The point here is not that a successful adoption of science and technology in Africa required the fulfilment of these conditions. Rather, we are making the claim that given the fact that the social setting was and continues to be different from seventeenth and eighteenth century Europe, science and technology are bound to impact Africa in a different way. Moreover, it seems to us important to remark that while in Europe science and technology were not necessarily viewed as foreign imports, even if one makes allowances for imports from the Far and Near East. In Africa, however, they are not only viewed as foreign imports, but also present themselves as such given the weaker ability of African countries to produce the goods of science and technology. As we will see further below, this is a significant point. It would be fair to argue in this connection that precisely differences in context account for differences in scientific cultures across the world. Therefore, we contend that difference in context, particularly on account of the fact that science and technology went to Africa as a turnkey project, yields a completely different starting point from the one which was experienced in Europe. Accordingly, a change of perspective seems to be required. It is perhaps useful to frame our question precisely around the foreign nature of science and technology and, more specifically, to inquire into the extent to which science and technology can be conceptualised as world views. The idea is to retrieve our initial concern with analysing the conditions under which individuals and communities respond to what they know in a context within which they may be confronted with different accounts of the natural world. In other words, we aim at finding out how foreign world views are assessed, rejected, adapted or changed and appropriated. This calls for a focus on reception.

The assertion of a frame of reference: the hegemony of interpretation

The starting point is the triad of material world, conceptual constructions and institutions. Generally speaking, in industrialised societies of the North an important part of socialisation is discharged by institutions that take the scientific-technological frame of reference for granted. Major exceptions in this regard are, of course, religious fundamentalists such as the "intelligent design" movement in the USA which seems to have been extremely successful there in challenging the authority of science, particularly as far as the teaching of Darwin's theory of natural selection in schools is concerned. These exceptions notwithstanding, much of everyday seems to be infused with wisdom that claims the authority of science for its validity. Children are socialised into this wisdom even before they enter formal schooling. Explanations by parents, in kindergarten or special children's television programmes reproduce scientific wisdom which carries within it a very specific interpretation of the world. A very good example in Germany is a well-known television programme called "Die Sendung mit der Maus" (The Mouse Show – our translation, DN, EM). This programme explains technology and basic facts of science in short movies and experiments. In this way, science as key to the material world is made to become a truism. Furthermore, schools present the world in subjects according to such scientific disciplines as geography, physics, chemistry and biology and our world is interpreted in scientific terms.

This does not imply that small children, pupils or adults truly understand all scientific explanations. Even reasonably well-educated sociologists are hardly able to pursue or understand biotech experiments. For most sociologists the mere challenge of clearing a bug from a computer system can be a daunting task. At the same time, however, we explain the world with reference to scientific theories. Simplified (or vulgarised) scientific theories become highly plausible. Indeed, there is a sense in which in industrialised societies such as those that can be found in Europe and North America science has become the standard against which the plausibility of accounts of the world is checked. This is not only due to the strength of its theories and knowledge. It is also due to the fact that scientific reasoning is backed by the powerful institutional apparatus of the state which in the event of conflicts over the interpretation of the world swings its weight in favour of science. Individuals may be inclined to argue with reference to religion or to eccentric or bizarre frames of reference, but if their claims are not consistent with science on matters of fact they are unlikely to hold sway. As a matter of fact, only a small group of experts is able to describe the world according to positivist science. More often than not their knowledge and expertise is specialised, which means that some are able to speak truthfully about a well-defined body of knowledge, while others concern themselves with other areas. However, their interpretation dominates public discussion and thinking, especially in its reference to the tenets of a scientific world view. To grasp the pervasive nature of science one could take the example of the debate on global warming. Global warming has become a truism, in spite of the fact that neither the journalists who report on it, nor the people in general who position themselves in relation to it, really understand the finer details of the matter. There are, of course, controversies surrounding the issue, particularly with regard to the extent of the problem and the political economy underlying public alarmist talk. Some people may even criticise the calculations of the complex studies on climate change. And some of those who level such criticism in public may not even be able to conduct research themselves. However, scientific data and assumptions underlie these debates, so much so that agreement and disagreement is achieved on the back of shared assumptions about the nature of the natural world which, in turn, are scientific in their substance.

This is not to claim that the scientific-technological frame of reference is the only frame of reference in Western societies. There are religious and there are also esoteric explanations of the world. While the scientific-technological frame of reference may be challenged, it (still) dominates everyday discourse in Western societies. The example of discourses on floods in the US Bible Belt mentioned above is a case in point. Scientists can lay claims to having been able to successfully claim epistemological hegemony for the production of knowledge (Kloppenburg 1991). Epistemological hegemony means the ability to assert one's standards of knowledge, what is to count as knowledge and knowledge validity over a society, a community or even a social group. Science in industrialised countries is seen as the most effective way to rationally interpret the world for the purposes of transforming it through technology. This belief in the superiority of science as far as the technological mastery of nature is concerned is what we call the interpretive hegemony of the scientific-technological frame of reference (Neubert & Macamo 2005). In making this claim we would like to point out that our perspective is sociological. Interpretive hegemony is achieved not only on the basis of the material success of a body of knowledge, but also on the basis of social and cultural resources which are arrayed in favour of a particular interpretation of the world. More often than not, interpretive hegemony is, therefore, directly linked to institutions which enforce the particular way of thinking fostered by the interpretation.

Scientists point out that they produce empirical evidence for their theories. This is important, but as we have learnt, empirical evidence is linked to specific constructions which are embedded into specific institutions. The floods may be interpreted along the scientific-technical "how" question concerning rainfall and dam management; or they may be interpreted along the "why" question concerning good or bad behaviour of the community. In both cases, the flood or its absence is seen as empirical data. Therefore, the scientific-technological frame of reference cannot convince just by experiments or isolated events. Societal legitimisation does seem to require at least two elements. One is the predictive ability of the underlying theories which supports the underlying frame of reference (Elwert 1995: 216). The other is the practical usefulness of technological artefacts to everyday life. The development of cars, cell phones, or aircrafts fulfils this expectation. Everyday life practice is a kind of social filter through which scientific-technological knowledge must pass in order to gain social acceptance. This is, as indicated above, coupled with other factors, such as cultural norms, social mores and perhaps even political circumstances which come together to socially produce the usefulness of technological artefacts. To put this differently, it is important to acknowledge the importance of practical usefulness. This makes technological artefacts attractive to individuals and communities. At the same time, though, practical usefulness is the outcome of the structure of society and the nature of social relations underlying it. As science and technology studies have shown, usefulness is socially constructed and as such it should not be conflated with the properties of technological artefacts (see the essays in Bijker & Law 1994 and in Law 1991).

To sum up, the scientific-technological frame of reference accomplishes interpretive hegemony on the basis of three interlinked elements:

- the utility of its products,
- reliability and institutions of assertion (Neubert & Macamo 2005) and
- the plausibility and the predictive ability of the theoretical models.

Products of modernity and expert systems

Against this background we may now take a fresher look at Africa. How does the scientific-technological frame of reference present itself there?

This frame of reference is part and parcel of "modernity".[8] By modernity we draw from Giddens (Giddens 1990), Eisenstadt (Eisenstadt 2000a, Eisenstadt 2000b) and Wittrock (Wittrock 2000) to understand a historical period marked by a specific structural figuration which had its origin as well as initial development in Europe. Subsequently this figuration spread all over the world. Modernity is characterised by a qualitatively new relationship among people and between them and nature. This relationship manifests itself in special political and societal projects as well as in the technological mastering/dominion over nature.

At the local level modernity as such or the dynamic structural figuration with its driving forces and institutional dimensions is usually not an issue. People are fascinated by specific things or ideas that create a desire and which, once there, have an effect on everyday life. Modernity promises welfare based on the comforts of technology, but also secured through the observation of certain values that are often thought to go along with a market based economic system. One has in mind the values of freedom, democracy and, more generally, human rights. Whether or to what extent the material and ideational aspects of modernity are activated by individuals and communities is a moot point. While modern technologies may promise a more comfortable life with more affluence and the emancipatory project of freedom, democracy and human rights may herald a more just society, there is no way of settling beforehand how individuals and

[8] The following paragraph is based on Macamo & Neubert 2008.

communities will engage modernity. They respond to it in their own terms, which is to say that local context, histories and the nature of the encounter with the outside world will shape the manner in which they will appropriate modernity. Whatever the case, we think that it is important to draw attention to the fact that what makes modernity such a powerful social factor is the fact that it challenges individuals and communities to engage it. In responding to it, individuals and communities may unleash processes of social change that should actually be placed at the centre of studies of the nature of social reality in Africa. While not stressing the notion of modernity, the French sociologist Georges Balandier was one of the first to acknowledge the importance of defining the object of sociological analysis along these lines. The work of the Rhodes Livingstone Institute in Zambia (former Northern Rhodesia) can also be subsumed under this research interest (for a useful review see Ferguson 1999).

One crucial analytical consequence that we draw from the discussion of the role of science and technology in everyday life and the nature of modernity is the suggestion that we seek to understand processes of change in local lifeworlds on the basis of how individuals and communities deal with the material and ideational artefacts that ensue modernity, but also how these artefacts impact local settings. We call these artefacts "products of modernity". Our path of inquiry bears specifically on the expert systems on which they are based and the kinds of structural conditions which they help to produce and come to bear on everyday life.

Products of modernity are material and ideational; they consist of:

- industrial products and the aspects of industrial processes themselves,
- (other) science based techniques, processes and knowledge (e.g. in medicine, agriculture, communication),
- secular ideas and ideologies like emancipatory societal projects or totalitarianism.

To be sure "products of modernity" should not be seen as being synonymous with Western or Northern. The origin of a product does not tell us anything about whether a product is modern or not. There are Southern products of modernity like software programmed in India, computer components designed and produced in China and there are products of the "West" that are globally available without being products of modernity like crafted glass from Venice. It is important to stress that "products of modernity" are an analytical shorthand description for a very particular form of knowledge that requires very particular expertise and social context for its production, dissemination and use. In some important respects, even if people are not interested in modernity as such, modernity may become relevant to people's lives through the intensive use and appropriation of its artefacts. Modernity, as Zygmunt Bauman (1991) once remarked upon, is an immanent phenomenon. It permeates social life in ways which are not directly retrievable by individuals in their everyday life. One way in which modernity achieves this immanence is through the attraction exercised by its artefacts over individuals. The trouble with these artefacts, however, is that they are like a "Trojan horse"; once people try to use them even on their own terms these may unleash far-reaching social consequences, most of which bear on the division of labour, social mobility, questioning of authority and the like.

Most of all, access to products of modernity places people at the risk of becoming dependent on their use. One aspect of this dependence is the difficulty of foregoing the comforts brought to one's life by products of modernity. There is a marked difference between walking or taking a bush taxi to the next village. Once one takes a bush taxi the distance becomes exceedingly long if one has to cover it on foot. Equally, enjoying freedom only to see it curtailed by the next coup d'état makes the former much more desirable than if one had never experienced it. Another aspect of the dependence relates to how the presence of products of modernity requires individuals and communities to create the conditions that are necessary for them to be properly used. These often refer to the technical capabilities, skills and perhaps even the legal institutions within the framework of which products of modernity function.

Especially complex material products of modernity in the form of technological artefacts are not only the result of complicated processes of research and development and elaborate systems of production, but they are also demanding in their use. One may not have the industrial plants that are required for their production, but to use them one needs certain skills (for example some level of literacy in the case of mobile phones), infrastructure (electricity) and perhaps even a legal framework (for the protection of privacy, etc.). Ultimately, products of modernity require for their protracted use what Giddens calls expert systems (Giddens 1990). In expert systems, expert knowledge is integrated within a complex institutional network and works continuously. Such systems ensure that the products are operated and can be maintained. Health centres and drug distribution systems are necessary for the use of modern medicine. The appropriate knowledge is held by experts only. The remaining members of society can only assume the effects of this knowledge, as they trust the underlying expert knowledge. Expert systems constitute a completely new set of institutions, including institutions for training and schooling. They create numerous new social positions and roles. The institutional network that backs the scientific-technological frame of reference mentioned by Latour is an expert system in Giddens' sense.

It is through the presence of an expert system that products of modernity insinuate themselves into local settings as a world view. They accomplish this feat through the requirement they place on individuals on opt for action that is consistent with the type of work which they assume. An individual who seeks bio-medical assistance may not understand the chemical composition of a prescribed drug. He may even fail to understand the exact details of the ailment that requires the type of treatment foreseen for him by the doctor. Using the drug and taking the treatment are two actions which are indifferent to whatever else an individual may feel to be the cause of his ailment, be it metaphysical or esoteric. Furthermore, drugs are to be taken according to clear schedules and rules which are self-sufficient and constrain the individuals' room for manoeuvre. This particular characteristic of products of modernity makes the underlying expert systems extremely insidious in their effects on everyday life, for they effectively challenge whatever perspectives may be available to individuals in coping with their everyday life. This is where products of modernity induce a clash between the expert systems which sustain them and the local world views that inform the social action of local individuals and communities.

Before we continue, let us tease out the analytical elements of our discussion so far. We have been concerned in this article with arguing that social action takes place in settings that are local and are informed by world views which give individuals a form of orientation in their everyday life. World views can be of several types and the scope of their validity can vary starting from local to global. While individuals may have a choice of frames of reference in deciding how to structure their everyday life, decisions concerning such choices may be influenced by the outcome of a conflict between competing world views. Over the past decades African local settings have been besieged by technological artefacts. In our view, the nature of these artefacts is crucial to understanding the texture of social action in local settings, particularly as they challenge conventional ways of thinking about the world. In the preceding chapters we have tried to show what is specific about these technological artefacts by articulating them with modernity and, in so doing, reducing their theoretical importance to the idea of expert systems as it was developed by Anthony Giddens. An important feature of these expert systems consists in their dialectical nature, i.e. the extent to which they jealously require action to follow from whatever account of the world they assume. We assume that the analytical relevance of products of modernity derives from this requirement and how it is perceived locally. In fact, in the introduction to the paper we indicated that we were puzzled by an apparent contradiction shown by peasants in the Limpopo valley who provided a scientific-technical account of the flood, but did not act upon it. They preferred to act according to their own wisdom. We also remarked that inhabitants of the Tennessee valley in America gave religious accounts of the disaster which they experienced, but acted according to scientific-technical rationality. Our hypothesis is that this apparent contradiction is related to the extent of scientific-technical impregnation of everyday life.

Products of modernity and the relevance of the "how" question

Let us now apply this analytical framework to our initial empirical findings. The combination of dykes, water management in dams with systematic data collection for whole river catchments is a technical product of modernity in which technical constructions for the use of and protection from water are linked into a complex information system. This constitutes a specific expert system. The use of these technological artefacts in the present context, particularly with regard to liberal democratic politics, is embedded in a normative framework that places a premium on the protection of human life. It holds government or, at any rate, authorities accountable for ensuring that appropriate action is taken to protect human life bearing in mind that appropriate action in this connection is action that is consistent with the assumptions underlying the expert system. Moreover, the presence of this particular product of modernity forces upon individuals a cruel choice between adopting it whole or being selective at the risk of futility.[9]

This system is available in the US Tennessee valley and in the Mozambique Limpopo valley, too. However, the everyday life experience with technical expert systems of the farmers in the Limpopo valley and the inhabitants of the Tennessee valley differs widely. It differs in the senses we discussed above, namely their utility, reliability and assertion and additionally plausibility and the predictive ability of the theoretical models.

In the Tennessee Valley all products of modernity are an integral part of the everyday life and their utility is taken for granted. Their presence has a long history and Americans, just like many other nationalities, seem to be proud of technological development and the spread of artefacts. In the event of problems experts are at hand for repair. Being an electrician, motor mechanic, TV-technician or a plumber is an ordinary trade like being a farmer. Therefore, many people are part of a particular expert system, which not only fosters a certain trust in the reliability of the products and supports the use of the scientific-technological frame of reference, but leaves little choice for alternatives which are not sanctioned by the general world view implied by science. In everyday life we find a basic do-it-yourself knowledge concerning the products of modernity. Technology has taken hold of life completely by way of the reliability of its artefacts and the institutional environment that expects individuals to refer to it. This, in turn, fosters the expectation that nature can be dominated by adequate technology leading to trust in its artefacts.

Based on this experience, coping with floods in this region is a technical matter quite apart from the more religious or metaphysical issue of knowing "why" things happen to people. Once products of modernity take hold of the everyday life and the supporting expert systems are part of normality the "Trojan horse" has accomplished its task. When this takes place the scientific-technological frame reference has the upper-hand in interpretation. Even when

9 Complex systems of water management existed long before modernity, e.g. irrigation systems for the cultivation of rice in Asia often combined with dykes for flood control. However, large dams for the running of hydro-power generators like on upstream Limpopo are a modern technical product as is the information system computing data from the whole Limpopo river and weather reports. The results of that information system led to the flood warning that was ignored by the people.

from a Christian fundamentalist point of view basic scientific notions of evolution might be criticised, in everyday life the matter of course of technology is less challenged or, at any rate, less consequential for social action.

In our study in Patrice Lumumba village we found that the local life-world is punctuated by the presence of technological artefacts which range from electricity and electrical appliances (television sets, mobile phones, radios, etc.) through public utilities such as piped water, hospitals and bio-medical drugs to cars, bicycles, motorbikes and, not less importantly, modern state administration structures and norms. These are more or less the same products of modernity as we find in Tennessee. The difference lies in the role these technical products play in everyday life. Medical services, for example, are beset with the problem of a shortage of doctors, ill-prepared nurses, obsolete or broken medical equipment, shortage of drugs and bandages, run-down and unhygienic buildings and corrupt staff. The piped water system in Patrice Lumumba does not work properly, there are constant power cuts and should technical devices break down it is hard to find somebody who is able to repair them. Additionally, only a few people hold positions in an expert system and those doing so are usually unqualified with little or no education.

In contrast to the Tennessee Valley products of modernity stand for complicated access and unreliability and the reference to them in everyday life is not institutionally asserted. The announcements that this or that technology will control nature hardly proved true. Irrigation systems which were once constructed have fallen apart, new agricultural techniques did not prove their usefulness, and the new medical systems have brought – seen from the local perspective – new diseases like pneumonia, malaria and recently AIDS/HIV.[10] Due to the unreliability and the contested usefulness of technical products of modernity villagers cannot use them in order to make their lives more predictable. In a

[10] This does not mean that Africans are not able to handle technical devices. These devices are part of everyday life. There are examples like the use of diesel engines by Sudanese farmers or the local refurbishment and reconstruction of Bedford trucks in Sudan (Beck 2001, 2004). But these products are isolated and the expert system, which in industrial countries is used for the development, production and maintenance of the product, is still missing. In cases like this the technical device is separated from its expert system and appropriated into the local frame of reference. The usability of these devices hardly supports the trustworthiness of the scientific-technical frame of reference.

nutshell, these technological products of modernity are less than relevant for local agency.

This influences the way people understand the world. An example should suffice to illustrate the point. In the case of a water fountain that was out of order villagers explained that a local spirit had not been consulted on the decision to dig the well on his land and, consequently, he had switched off the water supply. The villagers had already endeavoured to carry out the necessary ceremonies, but it was proving difficult because of the resistance of newcomers. Visiting technicians from the water authority, however, immediately found out that the reason why no water came out was that the local technician, who had only some basic training in maintenance, had installed the filter the wrong way when too much sand had blocked the pipe and he had been forced to repair it. This local explanation is again centred around the "why" question as in the case of the flood. Our point here is not that villagers are irrational in any essential way. Rather, as long as the types of frames of reference they use locally help them make reasonable claims and frame their interpretation of the world in a locally understandable way they will get away with it.

As long as products of modernity do not show their reliability and usefulness the frame of reference which is behind them cannot make an impact on people's everyday habits. If nature cannot be dominated, then the powers of nature have to be calmed. The control of local behaviour according to moral rules seems the more efficient way to escape further threats than to build on the unreliable products of modernity. However, if people are forced to relate their claims and their understanding of the world to another frame of reference, in this case, the scientific-technological one, they will have no choice but to conform, even if deep down they are not convinced. If such pressures on them to conform include consistent appeals to personal technical responsibility as the only grounds for whatever claims for assistance they wish to lay, then they will have no other choice. In fact, the situation is no different in societies impregnated with the scientific-technological rationality. Here we can even make a radical claim: the scientific-technological rationality does not depend on people understanding it for them to conform to it. Most people in the West do not understand it. All that it takes is habit. And habit comes with reliability and, often, force exercised by the state.

Conclusion

In this article we wanted to present a conceptual framework that helps us to analyse the relationship between social action and world views. Starting from our empirical example we wanted to understand under what conditions world views become determinant for action and, more specifically, why the scientific-technical world view is more relevant in the US than in Mozambique. We draw from a constructivist perspective, but respectful of the materiality of the world and experience, and, furthermore, sensitive to social change and its impact on local life-worlds.

Whereas from a natural-science point of view the conceptual constructions and the knowledge produced using these constructions are the core element, from an everyday life point of view the most important are the usability or benefit of the products which, however, are based on expert systems. From a social science point of view, the institutions are the most interesting, because first, they are the prerequisite that the products and through them the conceptual construction are ingrained in a society. Second, the development of expert systems restructures the society as a whole and is linked to what sociologists address under the heading of on-going differentiation.

Our point is twofold.

First of all, we argue that world views matter in any consideration of local agency. The way they matter is by providing a context within which the things which people do in their everyday life acquire meaning and can be analysed. At the same time world views are not isolated, they only become powerful in a triad of conceptual constructions, of usability or benefit of products developed using the conceptual constructions and institutions, which carry the concepts and stabilise the usability of products. The struggle for interpretive hegemony between the scientific-technological and the religious-magical frames of reference is decided in everyday life and not in a scholarly seminar.

Secondly, we have tried to make the point that processes of globalisation inhere into local life-worlds through world views or, to be more precise, frames of reference which constrain local agency. More often than not it is the confrontation between frames of reference which decides the nature and character of processes of globalisation at the local level.

References

Antweiler, Christoph (1998): Local Knowledge and Local Knowing. An Anthropological Analysis of Contested 'Cultural Products' in the Context of Development. *Anthropos* 93/1998, 469-494.

Bauman, Zygmunt (1991): *Modernity and Ambivalence*. Ithaca, N.Y.: Cornell University Press.

Beck, Kurt (2001): Die Aneignung der Maschine. Eine Geschichte, die davon handelt wie der Dieselmotor von Bauern im Niltal so gezähmt und zugerichtet wurde, daß er aus seiner neuen Heimat nicht mehr wegzudenken ist. In: Kohl, Karl-Heinz (ed.): *New Heimat*. New York: Lukas & Sternberg, 66-77.

— (2004): Bedfords Metamorphose. In: Beck, Kurt, Till Förster and Hans Peter Hahn (eds.): *Blick nach vorn. Festgabe für Gerd Spittler*. Köln: Rüdiger Köppe Verlag, 250-264.

Bellinger, Andréa and David J. Krieger (eds.) (2006): *ANThology. Ein einführendes Handbuch zur Akteur-Netzwerk-Theorie*. Bielefeld: Transcript.

Bijker, Wiebe E. and John Law (eds.) (1994): *Shaping Technology / Building Society: Studies in Sociotechnical Change*. Cambridge: MIT Press.

Bonß, Wolfgang and Heinz Hartmann (eds.) (1985): Entzauberte Wissenschaft. *Soziale Welt: Sonderband 3*. Göttingen: Scharz.

Christie, Frances and Joseph Hanlon (2001): *Mozambique and the Great Flood of 2000*. Bloomington: Indiana University Press.

Eisenstadt, Shmuel Noah (2000a): Multiple Modernities. *Daedalus, Journal of the American Academy of Arts and Science* 129 (1): Multiple Modernities, 1-30.

— (2000b): *Die Vielfalt der Moderne*. Weilerswist: Velbrück Wissenschaft.

Elwert, Georg (1995): Changing Certainties and the Move to a 'Global' Religion. Medical Knowledge and Islamization among Anii (Baseda) in the Republic of Bénin. In: Wendy James (ed.): *The Pursuit of Certainty. Religious and Cultural Formulations*. London: Routledge, 215-233.

Ferguson, James (1999): *Expectations of Modernity: Myths and Meanings of Urban Life on the Zambian Copperbelt*. Berkeley: University of California Press.

Giddens, Anthony (1990): *The Consequences of Modernity*. Stanford: Stanford University Press.

Goffman, Erving (1980): *Rahmen-Analyse. Ein Versuch über die Organisation von Alltagserfahrungen*. Frankfurt/M.: Suhrkamp.

Kloppenburg, Jack (1991): Social Theory and the De/Reconstruction of Agricultural Science: Lokal Knowledge for an Alternative Agriculture. *Rural Sociology* 56 (4), 519-548.

Knorr-Cetina, Karin (1999): *Epistemic Cultures. How the Sciences Make Knowledge*. Cambridge, Mass. and London: Harvard University Press.

Latour, Bruno (1984): *The Pasteurization of France*. Cambridge, Mass.: Harvard University Press.

— (1993): *We Have Never Been Modern*. Cambridge, Mass.: Harvard University Press.

Law, John, (ed.) (1991): *A Sociology of Monsters: Essays on Power, Technology and Domination*. London: Routledge.

Loimeier, Roman, Dieter Neubert and Cordula Weißköppel (eds.) (2005): Globalization in the Local Context. Perspectives and Concepts of Action in Africa. An Introduction. *Bayreuth African Studies Online* 2. Bayreuth: Institut für Afrikastudien & Kulturwissenschaftliches Forschungskolleg (SFB/FK 560).

Macamo, Elísio and Dieter Neubert (2008): The New and its Temptations. Products of Modernity and their Impact on Social Change in Africa. In: Adogame, Afe, Magnus Echtler and Ulf Vierke (eds.): *Unpacking the New. Rethinking Cultural Syncretization in Africa and Beyond*. Münster, Hamburg, Berlin: LIT Verlag, 271-303.

— (in print): 'Flood Disasters'. A Sociological Analysis of Local Perception and Management of Extreme Events based on Examples from Mozambique, Germany, and the USA. In: Ute Luig (ed.): *Disaster Politics: Coping Strategies, Representations and Memory*. Frankfurt/M.: Lang.

Neubert, Dieter and Elísio Macamo (2005): Wer weiß hier was? 'Authentisches' lokales Wissen und der Globalisierungsanspruch der Wissenschaft. In: Loimeier, Roman, Dieter Neubert and Cordula Weißköppel (eds.): *Globalisierung im lokalen Kontext. Perspektiven und Konzepte von Handeln in Afrika*. Münster: LIT Verlag, 237-275.

Plough, Alonzo and Sheldon Krimsky (1987): The Emergence of Risk Communication Studies: Social and Political Context. *Science, Technology and Human Values* 12 (3/4), 4-10.

Scott, James C. (1998[4]): *Seeing like a State: How Certain Schemes to Improve the Human Condition have Failed.* New Haven and London: Yale University Press.

Searle, John (1995): *The Construction of Social Reality.* New York: The Free Press.

von Glasersfeld, Ernst (1995): *Radical Constructivism: A Way of Knowing and Learning.* London: The Falmer Press.

Walzer, Michael (1994): *Thick and Thin: Moral Argument at Home and Abroad.* London: University of Notre Dame Press.

Wittrock, Björn (2000): Modernity: One, None, or Many? European Origins and Modernity as a Global Condition. *Daedalus, Journal of the American Academy of Arts and Science* 129 (1): Multiple Modernities, 31-60.

Agency in Africa: The Domestication of the Modern Mind

Patrick Chabal

The matter of agency in Africa, which has become increasingly salient, is at the intersection of issues that raise a number of fundamental historical and conceptual questions. Why should there now be greater concern with African agency than there was in any of the previous decades since independence? Why indeed should the notion of agency have acquired such a prominent place in the social science discourse on Africa? What, in any event, does agency mean or, perhaps more concretely, how does the concept help us better to understand African realities at the beginning of the twenty-first century? What, if any, are the connections between the focus on agency and the rise of an international anti-globalisation movement?

For the sake of simplifying what is a complex set of issues, I have focussed here on two main questions:

1. Has the use of a new discourse to conceptualise Africa's relations with the outside (global) world revealed new processes and new forms of action that were neglected or misconstrued by analysis before?
2. Has the supposedly different context of current globalisation actually resulted in novel and substantively different agency on the ground in Africa?

This article is in three unequal parts. The first discusses the genealogy and relevance of the concept of agency currently used in the social sciences. The second seeks to anchor this discussion in the African historical context. The third, longest, section attempts to answer the two questions above by means of an analysis of the intricate inter-relationships between history, politics, culture and language in the study of Africa over time.

I will conclude that the question of the renewed attention given to the urgency of agency in Africa in light of an apparently totalising process of globalisation is in fact an argument about an old question: what is the place of Africa in the contemporary world?

The importance presently given to the concept of agency in contemporary African Studies has its roots in two distinct genealogies. The first has to do with a number of shifts in the social sciences since the sixties. The second is linked to the evolving situation in Africa, which most analysts frame today in terms of the impact of globalisation on the continent. I discuss them in turn.

Of concepts and discourses

Agency is usually understood as directed, meaningful, intentional and self-reflective social action. It is not possible here to trace in full the genealogy of this notion since this would involve a systematic discussion of paradigm shifts in several key social sciences. Suffice it to say that it comes out of a longstanding debate about the respective importance of structure and agency.[1]

The dominance after the Second World War of Marxist, neo-Marxist, teleological or structuralist approaches to the study of society began to be questioned in the sixties. However, it was not until the seventies that its supremacy was challenged. Michel Foucault and Jürgen Habermas, each in his very different epistemological manner, initiated a number of critiques, which were eventually to change the face of the social sciences. More concretely, it also began to influence the way Africanists went about their business.

One must consider at least two important shifts in both history and the social sciences, which had a deep impact on the question of agency. On the one hand, the rise of cultural history and the linguistic turn led to a complete reassessment of history. This has opened up a vast transformation in the "theory" of history, particularly in areas such as feminism and the study of the non-Western world. On the other hand, the social sciences themselves underwent a double shift: the historical turn and the linguistic turn. These have brought about a focus on subjectivity, discourse and deconstruction.

The challenge to structuralism and teleology, in history and the social sciences, inevitably recast the question of agency as well as the matter of causality – two topics to which I now turn.

The move away from the structural determinant of social action took a long time and proceeded unevenly. As far as African Studies are concerned, the sixties and seventies were a period during which theories of (economic and politi-

[1] I cannot discuss the origins and complexity of the concept of agency here as it is now used in Africanist social sciences. The reader is encouraged to consult the following: Archer 2003; Lonsdale 2000; Ortner 2006; van Binsbergen & van Dijk 2004.

cal) development combined to suggest that the putting in place of the right structures and the execution of the right policies would result in progress. The disagreements concerned the question of whether capitalism or socialism was the most powerful engine of modernisation.

Whether capitalist or socialist, the notions deployed all took for granted the fact that agency was directly conditioned by the economic, political and social constraints extant in each particular society and within the global economic order. The question was not, therefore, whether different agency might result in different outcomes but how agency could best be applied to the work of purposeful social action within the structural framework that determined the range of possible options. Agency, then, was subordinated to structure within the context of an understanding of historical causality that brooked little dissent.

The move away from such a conceptual framework began to gather momentum in the seventies but the particular situation of Africa prevented this shift from having decisive analytical purchase until the eighties. Perhaps the delayed entry of the notion of agency onto the African scene is linked to the sense of urgency with which it is deployed today: there is a need to catch up! However, as I shall show below, there is more than a hint of ambiguity in the concept of agency as it is used today in the study of Africa.

Although the gradual emergence of a discourse of agency masks any clear epistemological break, it is important to set it in some historical context. It is in fact the fall of the Berlin Wall along with the collapse of communism in the Soviet Union and Eastern Europe, which helped to bring back subjectivity and agency in the analysis of social and political action. For example, the modern resurgence of civil society as a social entity with decisive influence on the political transformation of modern societies issues more or less directly from an analysis of the East European transitions to democracy that gives pride of place to agency.

The post-communist context enabled the flowering of theories of modernisation, which placed the strong individualism of liberal democracy and the decisive role of the market at the heart of political and economic change – in Africa as in the rest of the world. It is within this setting that democratisation washed over Africa and began to re-define the terms of the discussion on development. Agency is in this way the link between democracy and the market, both of which privilege an analysis of society in terms of the empowered individual endowed with social, political and economic rights.

Africa: the historical context

The situation in Africa at the time when the entwined discourses on democracy and market gained ascendancy was that of extreme crisis. Indeed, the late eighties marked the point at which the dereliction of the continent was so great that doubts were raised about its future development. At the same time, the end of the Cold War and the concern in the West for the evolution of the former communist states made it much more difficult for African countries to get the foreign aid on which their very survival depended. So it was that a fundamental rethinking of the African predicament began to take shape. So it was too that the discourse about Africa began to change.

The recognition of the limited success (or outright failure) of the benign "paternalism" that had presided over the imposition of structural adjustment programmes – the thinking being that African governments had to be taught how to manage their economy for the purpose of development – went hand in hand with a new vision of African agency. This vision had its origins in two separate though clearly interrelated processes.

One was the extent of social mobilisation that was said to have led to the revolt against the one-party state and ushered in competitive politics in most African countries. This hinted both at the powerful effects of "civil society" as a key driver of change and at the potential for positive transition inherent in democracy. The other was the realisation that there were myriad social, economic and political "informal" activities that demonstrated the ability of Africans to survive the catastrophic conditions under which they were compelled to live. This extraordinary dynamism and ingenuity suggested that, once the heavy hand of the state had been removed there would be scope for genuine developmental progress.

Since the early nineties, therefore, there has emerged a two-strand discourse on agency. One has tapped into the new aid ideology of providing support to civil society at the local level – a role devolved to (foreign and domestic) NGOs. The other has linked with the idea that development would have to come through the combined efforts of individuals: informal ingenuity would have to be channelled into formal productive activities that would sustain economic growth. This largely foreign vision of the new Africa was reinforced by the discourse of African politicians who now berated the failures of the one-party state model of development and promised to facilitate both political reform and market-friendly policies.

The new discourse on Africa was sealed in two key documents at the turn of the century: NEPAD and the Millennium Development Goals (MDG) – one the mirror image of the other. The sub-text was clear: help thyself and the world will help you. The new dispensation was thus predicated on the force of agency: directed African action would, with the help of the outside world, lay down the basis for greater political accountability, more development and the reduction of poverty. The G8 summit in 2005 finalised this compact between Africans and donors.

Yet another powerful strand in the genealogy of agency has been the need, among Africans and Africanists alike, to counter the mood of Afro-pessimism, which descended over the continent in the eighties and has not lifted since. Many hoped to move away from the perspective of Africa as a "victim" and give pride of place to African "initiative". This was a deliberate attempt to oppose those approaches that stressed the structural features of African societies, most particularly neo-patrimonialism, as being the main explanatory factors for the on-going crisis. The analytical claim made by those who favoured agency was that a focus on what was being achieved, instead of what had failed, would highlight the local ways in which African actors had managed to cope with the twin burden of weak/failed states and the pressures of globalisation. Centring attention on agency would change the questions we asked about African societies. As a recent article explains:

> Over the past four decades, all the major social-science paradigms from structuralism to Marxism, world-systems theory and globalization that sought to explain the predicament of African societies in terms of structure have been countered and critiqued by perspectives that emphasised human creativity and resilience, in other words 'agency'. One of the important contributions of the agency perspective to the academic understanding of social change in Africa has been its capacity to explode […] victimizing approaches in exchange for a much more balanced understanding of the local processes at work in Africa (de Bruijn, van Dijk & Gewald 2007).

The notion of agency is thus not "neutral". It arises from a specific intellectual and historical context, which points to the limits of Africanist social sciences. Hence it is argued that existing paradigms have failed to explain contemporary Africa, casting it in an everlasting vicious circle of impotence. There is a perceived need to provide an analytical framework that does justice to the processes of social change actually taking place in Africa today.

Agency has now become a powerful concept, which informs not just scholarship but also policy making. It contributes to new approaches in development aid that have immediate consequences on the ground in Africa. And it is in this way in the process of becoming the new "orthodoxy" despite the warning given by some of those who advocate its use. The authors cited above explain that "the concept of agency runs counter to the idea of makeability and therefore counter to interventionist paradigms that assume the possibility of guided, if not mechanical, transformations of social realities … [whereas] agency is related to the unpredictability of outcomes of processes of change" (de Bruijn, van Dijk & Gewald 2007).

It is time to reflect upon both the notion of agency itself and its application to Africa as currently practised.

So what is new?

A closer look at the concept of agency in Africa reveals an ambiguity at its very core. On the one hand, the notion has arisen from epistemological changes in the social sciences, reflecting primarily Western, non-African, societies. On the other hand, it has emerged from the ground up as a category of analysis for the local African context. Although the word used is the same, it carries vastly different implications. The former centres on the fact that in "modern" societies the individual is deemed to be more of a "free" agent than in so-called "traditional" societies. The very condition of "modernity" is taken to be the vastness of the possibilities of social and political action. The latter suggests the ability of African men and women to adapt to and process modernity for their own purposes.

Of course, it is recognised in the literature about agency that the absence of resources and opportunities influences the extent to which African men and women are able to act upon the environment in which they live. It is also admitted that African societies are not primarily atomistic and individualised in ways that would put a premium on the individual's intentional, purposeful and autonomous social action. For all these reservations, however, the notion of agency has taken a firm hold on a large swathe of social and political analysis. It is almost as if the incantation of agency will eventually serve to create and develop a firmer sense of individual potentialities in Africa today.

So, how useful is the concept in the African context? I tackle this issue from two different angles. The first is to tease out the ways in which it forces us to ask different questions about what is happening on the continent. The second is to discuss the extent to which, as a mirror image of the notion of Afro-pessimism, it is inextricably bound with the causalities it seeks to undermine.

(i) There is little doubt that concentrating on agency forces us to (re)consider the main questions we've been asking since independence. Instead of raising the issue of why Africa has not developed, we are directed to consider the extraordinary ways in which Africans have adapted to a rapidly changing world order. From a context in the sixties when the Cold War was at its height and the formal colonial powers still had strong influence in their former territories to the present globalised world in which financial, communication and trade flows have accelerated, Africa's situation has evolved massively.

A focus on the adjustments Africans have had to make to confront these global influences brings out the ability of both rulers and peoples to grasp the opportunities available to them and deploy them to purposeful effect. A few examples will make the point. The agility demonstrated by African governments in maximising resource transfers within the radically different environments of the Cold War, then structural adjustment and, today, rapid globalisation is truly impressive. Equally, the speed at which Africans deployed the discourse and instruments of democracy to force greater accountability on their governors is remarkable. On another register, the ease with which Africans have adapted to the spread of the mobile phone and the internet to facilitate commerce and migration is nothing short of astonishing. By the same token, the so-called informal economies have thrived in and beyond Africa. Finally, the rapid development of local NGOs as well as the increasingly organised and vocal intervention of civil society organisations (CSOs) demonstrate the potential for "grassroots" organisations to influence politics.

Concentrating attention on what has contributed to major political, social and economic changes in the last decade forces analysts to think again about the instruments they use to explain these events and processes. I give three examples.

(a) There is now a new analytical framework that accounts for the patterns and consequences of African migration, which goes beyond the common assumption that African (e)migration involves primarily the movement of Africans towards the outside world. The sight of would-be-migrants drowning on their way to the Canaries or dying on the barbed wires of Ceuta reinforces the message from Western politicians that Europe is being swamped by African immigrants. In fact, this research shows that there are vast movements of peoples between African countries that drive a thriving continent-wide "informal" economy sustaining large numbers of people in many different countries. Patterns of intra-Africa emigration also contribute significantly to re-define territoriality on the continent.

(b) Asking how democratisation has worked in practice has brought out the need to study much more carefully what might be called "traditional" forms of political accountability. Recent work has shown the pointlessness of African society in terms of a dichotomy between "traditional" and "modern". It has led to a re-thinking of the notion of accountability so as to enable us to take into consideration the multifarious ways in which agency actually works on the ground. Some of the research suggests that in many complex ways the so-called "traditional" forms are more effective at turning "democracy" into a reality than the more formal institutional mechanisms presumed to ensure accountability. Or at least that the way in which the two interact is more intricate than standard political theory would allow.

(c) Studying how communities in Africa have faced up to the issues of violence, justice and reconciliation points to variegated forms of so-called "traditional" methods, which have in practice proved worthwhile. Ranging from the *gacaca* tribunals in Rwanda to the village-based cleansing ceremonies in Mozambique, there are on the continent numerous instances of informal methods by which communities address, deal with and resolve even the most unspeakable acts of violence or the most intractable causes of conflict. The interesting question here is precisely the overlapping of the formal and informal in a process of social and political transition that is firmly modern.

These advances in our understanding of African social and political action are important. They force us to revise any overall notion of causality we may have taken for granted by dint of the theoretical or conceptual frameworks we've been prone to use. There is certainly no doubt that any pre-conceived analytical scheme that does not allow for the study of the myriad instances of social action to be observed in contemporary Africa is likely to seriously distort our account of what is happening there.

However, there is also another side to the issue of agency, which I now want to examine.

(ii) The question here is whether the fact that the stress on agency is also an argument designed to rebut those approaches commonly labelled Afro-pessimist is analytically relevant. Just as it can be argued – though I have no time to take up this discussion here – that post-colonial theories are symbiotically bound with those they debunk, so it could be the case for an approach in terms of African agency.

From this angle, it seems to me that the stress on agency issues from two separate, though complementary, aspects of a particular approach to Africa. One is a deep and real concern that, contrary to the expectations of the early post-independence period, the continent has failed to develop. However this is to be explained, this situation demands an explanation. The other is the worry that globalisation, which is widely believed to have become the overriding factor in present world relations, is seriously detrimental to Africa – making it even less likely that the continent will be able finally to develop. I do not discuss either of these two issues in any detail but want to focus instead on how they interact in the construction of current discourses on Africa.

Explanations of the present situation in Africa fall into two, very unequal, categories.

The first lays the blame on historical, environmental or structural factors, which range from neo-colonialism to the nature of exports from the continent. Today, the main area of concern is globalisation. What these explanations all share is an emphasis on those conditions that affect Africa, which are outside local control: Africa is where it is because it suffers an unusually cruel combination of constraints. My point here is not to assess the relative merit of these factors, all of which are relevant, but to highlight the way in which they stress causes that lie beyond agency: Africa is the victim of circumstances. Thus, such discourses point to the helplessness of those who are fated to live in that part of the world.

Although concerns about globalisation today are clearly linked to the specific ways in which the world has been moving since the end of the Cold War, the discussion about globalisation has echoes from the past. Strangely, they encompass two opposite views, which were familiar in the sixties and early seventies debates about capitalist intrusion into Africa. Those who favoured a strong version of dependency theory (Samir Amin[2]) argued for detachment from the world market and autonomous economic development. Those who believed capitalism necessary (Bill Warren[3]) or desirable (World Bank economists) called for more multinational investment on the continent. That debate is not now at the top of the agenda but it has spawned a similar one about globalisation.

The anti-globalisation movement points out that current developments are not favourable to Africa – for two sets of reasons. One is that the continent, which is greatly dependent on agricultural exports, is heavily penalised by Western subsidies to their own farmers, subsidies which counter some of the efforts these countries have made to open up their markets to imports from Africa. The other is that multinationals are shunning Africa and investing elsewhere, thus depriving the continent of much needed capital and know-how. Africa is not benefiting from the supposed benefits of globalisation, which are essentially passing Africa by. What we have here is an argument in which the two types of explanation coalesce: globalisation is not good for Africa but even that aspect of it that could be beneficial is denied because economic interests only seek profits and Africa is not profitable. Again, the conclusion is that globalisation denies Africans agency.

The second explanation, which stresses political factors, evokes instead processes and events that are largely rooted internally. Without neglecting any of the problems caused by the continent's fundamental "extraversion", those who advocate a focus on the politics of Africa as the main cause of its crisis ask questions about the nature of accountability. Whether they speak of neo-patrimonialism or emphasise other political practices in Africa, they point to the

---

2 See, among others, Samir Amin (2010): *Global History: a View from the South*. Oxford: Pambazuka Press.

3 See Bill Warren (1980): *Imperialism: Pioneer of Capitalism*. London: Verso.

fact that the operation of political systems on the continent has failed to provide an environment within which it is possible for productive economic activities to flourish.

This second line of attack, emphasising as it does the responsibility of African elites, can take two different tacks and result, therefore, in two diverging, although interconnected, interpretations of politics in Africa. One is to argue that the present condition of African states is the result of the working out of historical processes in a local context – or what is sometimes called the historicising of the state. The argument is that the transplantation of the colonial state into an environment that was not propitious and the historical development of that state in the post-colonial context have resulted in a political system that merely serves the interests of the elites. The other is that the present dereliction of the state in Africa is the result of the working out of a perverse evolution of the "traditional" politics of Africa in the modern context of a continent that is sustained by outside aid. In other words, it is foreign assistance that makes it possible for the political elites to use the state in such patrimonial fashion in order to stay in power.

Whilst the standard account of the deleterious effects of elite behaviour in Africa stresses their greed and dishonesty, both the above interpretations point to the problem inherent in a political system that is blatantly adverse to sustained development. Both agree that the problem lies in a lack of real accountability but their diagnosis differs when it comes to agency. The first implies that the nature of politics in Africa is the result of the imposition of a foreign state that is not suited to local conditions and which has made possible the abuse of power. The second suggests that it is instead the transformation of political "traditions" within the post-colonial context that is at the heart of the problem. In the first account, Africa is still the victim of the foreign, colonial, intrusion. In the second, the responsibility lies more squarely with elites who have put in place a political system enabling them to use pseudo-traditional patrimonial forms of accountability to abuse their power.

It is this second interpretation that is most often linked with Afro-pessimism because it implies that the problem lies with the singular adaptation of "traditional" African forms of social and political relations to the modern world. And inevitably, the claim that it is the very socio-political and cultural foundations of African societies that may have the greater impact on the present crisis is taken to be an argument that the continent is fated never to manage to resolve its problems. This easily transmutes into the contention that the crisis is both inevitable and intractable, which implies that Africans lack agency – cursed as they are by their own institutions and traditions. Hence, much of the impetus for a focus on what Africans have achieved or can achieve autonomously derives from an attempt to combat the apparently fateful causalities of Afro-pessimism.

As a consequence, the emphasis on agency is frequently more an effort to combat a diagnosis that is disliked than a well-grounded endeavour to assess the extent to which local initiatives are in fact instances of systemic political and economic change. My point is obviously not to decry the very useful, and insightful, emphasis given to the multiple ways in which Africans cope with the very painful pangs of modernisation. It is instead to point to the fact that what lies behind the use of the notion of agency is rather more complicated than at first appears. Far from being an entirely novel conceptualisation of the advance made by Africans in the resolution of the crisis from which they suffer, agency is actually a way of saying that they manage to cope in the adverse circumstances of a systemic condition in which development is not really on the agenda.

From that viewpoint, the present focus on agency is a way of redeeming Africans from the demeaning situation in which the outside world has placed and kept them. Whilst it is understandable that Africanists should seek to explain how Africans are adapting and succeeding in the modern world – how indeed they are domesticating the modern mind – it is important to bear in mind that such a normative approach is by no means devoid of analytical risks. At the very least it raises questions which must be addressed. One is why we should stress agency in Africa more than we do in other settings. Another is whether Africans themselves see what they do as agency (I am reminded here of Wole Soyinka's quip about Léopold Sédar Senghor's Négritude: "Is the tiger concerned about its tigritude?").

Although I shall not answer these questions here I will make one final remark. Strangely enough, an excessive emphasis on agency could turn out to be yet another way of depriving Africans of agency insofar as it focuses attention on what they do to survive rather than on what they might do by way of achieving the kind of structural and systemic change that would eventually lead to self-sustained development. On that reading, the stress on agency could be seen as a new way of saying an old thing: Africans are not free to do what they want because of external factors (now, globalisation). If that is correct, then, it is potentially one more in a long litany of discourses on "victimhood" – all of which are in fact patronising since they point to the continued inability of Africans to take matters in their own hands beyond survival.

References

Amin, Samir (2010): *Global History: a View from the South*. Oxford: Pambazuka Press.

De Bruijn, Mirjam, Rijk van Dijk and Jan-Bart Gewald (2007): Social and Historical Trajectories of Agency in Africa. In: Chabal, Patrick, Ulf Engel and Leo de Haan (eds.): *African Alternatives*. Leiden: Brill, 9-20.

Archer, Margaret (2003): *Structure, Agency and the Internal Conversation*. Cambridge: Cambridge University Press.

Lonsdale, John (2000): Agency in Tight Corners: Narrative and Initiative in African History. In: *Journal of African Cultural Studies* 13 (1), 5-16.

Ortner, Sherry (2006): *Anthropology and Social Theory: Culture, Power and the Acting Subject*. Durham: Duke University Press.

Van Binsbergen, Wim and Rijk van Dijk (eds.) (2004): *Situating Globality: African Agency in the Appropriation of Global Culture*. Leiden: Brill.

Warren, Bill. (1980): *Imperialism: Pioneer of Capitalism*. London: Verso.

World Views and Social Actors: A Social Mechanisms Approach to Development Situations

Dieter Goetze

Introduction: approaching the question

At least since Max Weber called attention to the significant role of world views in the development of different aspects of this-worldliness of the great world religions and its implications for processes of rationalisation, sociological theory has taken for granted that social action and world views are intimately interrelated. But the precise meaning of this relationship has since then always been a matter open for debate, as even the Weberian argument ends up by admitting that the influence of world views on social action diminishes with the generalised establishment of formal rationality and the consequent rationalisation of the cognitive and normative background of (European) civilisation processes. One of the important consequences has been the near monopolisation of the concept by anthropology and, conversely, the relative neglect of the place of world views in sociological theory or, more precisely, the retreat of this aspect into a realm even beyond the dimension of normative embedding of social action. A good example for this procedure is Talcott Parsons' (1968, 1978) appreciation that world views belong to the diffuse general background that he called the "ultimate reality" and he therefore saw as only remotely connected to social action by offering a highly general framework of existential meanings, a sort of interpretative anthropological tapestry that could be compatible with a wide array of concrete ways of action and of classification of actors. In a similar way Peter L. Berger and Thomas Luckmann, the authors of "The social construction of reality", took great care to make clear that world views belong to the space where the production of meanings and knowledge takes place and from which the many different components of multiple constructed realities are taken. So, one of the prime tasks of this article will be to try to specify in detail the relationship of world views and the category of agency, as the call for papers for the conference preceding this book parts from the supposition that "world views as perspectives on the world" offer "interpretive frameworks [...] on the nature of reality [...that] are produced by agency, but also provide contexts within which agency unfolds" (CfP Conference). This presupposes a reflexive relationship between these two categories and this aspect deserves special attention.

In the second place, I will try to focus more precisely on the specific way in which the multiple processes of globalisation could be said to influence relevant world views. I will try to locate its influence in the context of "development", especially in view of some aspects that are conveyed by the dominant notions of globalisation. A critical look at this ample field will show that one has to be very careful with the analysis of the complex relationship of these notions with the different variations of social action. Possibly, many interdependencies are not really directly influenced by a specific world view, especially in the context of some situations defined by the social actors as situations of "development", but may be much better explained by the analytical category of "social mechanism". Therefore, I will try to go into the question of the relationship between agency and certain social mechanisms that may be influenced by new frameworks of meaning determined by globalisation processes. And finally, I will try to take a look at the ways and means by which we, nevertheless, may be able to analytically identify a concrete role for world views forming social agency in globalisation contexts. But the whole argument is led by the presupposition that, especially where interdisciplinary investigation could be useful, it should take place without giving up the explanatory intention of sociological analysis. This is of central importance in investigations on the interplay of world views and agency, as it helps to distinguish sociology from other conceptual approaches and any attempts to subsume its analytical efforts as just one more kind of narration of the social under the label of a generalised "social theory" (Goetze 2007).

The problem: world views and agency – a loosely structured relationship

I started my introduction by emphasising the relative neglect that the category of "world view" has suffered in sociological theory. That seems to stand in clear contrast to the evident anthropological interest in these matters, as especially the classical anthropological investigation that was centred on the "small community", frequently emphasised the part played by particular models of world view as limiting factors for social action. Famous in this respect became for instance George M. Foster's "image of limited good" (Foster 1979) or the "amoral familism" of Edward C. Banfield (1958). Both of them aimed mainly at the explanation of the relationship of peasant societies to a modern world supposedly characterised by a rather different interpretive framework for action. Its repertoire of meanings was considered to be oriented by a process of rationalisation, dominated by generalised ideas of material causality based on the human capacity of rational action, scientific knowledge and a shaping of reality according to its perceived productive needs. So, the relative neglect of the world view category by sociological theorising reflects a diffuse supposition also shared by anthropology: the idea that those particular world views were condemned to dissolve progressively, as they were confronted by this diffusely homogeneous and always more dominant general world view of modernity – they became "traditional". So this diminishing interest of sociology in the matter of different world views may well be caused by the generalised tendency to assume that modernity, especially in its Euro-American version, goes hand-in-hand with a reduced relevance of influences caused by particular world views. As generalised processes of rationalisation and "world-oriented" values diffuse, the practical activities "in the world" have themselves become infused with "ethical ideals" and – so at least has told us Max Weber – the rational orientations of social action are penetrated by practical-ethical dimensions. What Weber called the "loss of the magic spell" of the world ("Entzauberung") really amounts to the idea that a radical crumbling of the binding force of world views has taken place, giving way to a competitive relationship between highly abstract cognitive and ideational thrusts that have no ethically binding influence on action but whose acceptance depends on their relative success in practical action vis-à-vis other cognitive positions and ideas.[1]

I have deliberately taken reference to Weber's interpretation of the cognitive and value consequences of rationalisation processes in the West, because it is precisely the European history of ideas that has profoundly influenced the sociological and the anthropological analysis and interpretations of the concept of world views, especially its role in the polarised construction of "tradition" and "modernity". So, if we assume the binding normative force of a specific world view for social action under "non-modern" social conditions as evident because of its legitimating relationship to an other-worldly based ethic then, how can we

1 For details see Weber 1972, Kalberg 2003, Schluchter 1980.

analytically conceive the relationship of agency to different competing world views with specific inner-worldly and practical-ethical orientations of action?

It may be helpful to take a closer look at this category of agency that has become of central importance in modern social theory, especially in the theories of Anthony Giddens, Pierre Bourdieu or Margaret Archer,[2] to mention only some of the sociologists who have used it in their attempts to analyse the interpenetration of agency and structure, without paying enough attention to the intrinsic qualities of agency itself. A central feature of agency – and that may well be the most important result of the Giddens-Archer controversy – is that it is situated in a flow of time. More precisely and following the argument of Mustafa Emirbayer and Ann Mische (1998: 964), it can be said that agency is an "internally complex dynamic", that is informed by the past, oriented toward the future and also toward the present contingencies. In this perspective "agency" can be defined as "the temporally constructed engagement by actors of different structural environments – the temporal-relational contexts of action – which, through the interplay of habit, imagination, and judgment, both reproduces and transforms those structures in interactive response to the problems posed by changing historical situations" (Emirbayer & Mische 1998: 970). These authors have then proceeded to discern three elements which compose human agency – and all of them relate directly to the category of the world view: – the iterative element, in that actors reactivate past patterns of thought and action, that are a sediment of past experience incorporated in world views; – the projective element, in that actors imagine future trajectories of action and reconfigure received structures in relation to desired future results of action; – the practical-evaluative element, in that actors have the capacity to judge about alternative ways of action practically and normatively, taking into account evolving situational demands and circumstances (cf. Fig. 1, see Emirbayer & Mische 1998: 971).

[2] See esp. Giddens 1990, Archer 1995 and 1996, Bourdieu 1977 and 1990.

Agency
- Iterational element
- Projective element
- Practical-evaluative element

Fig. 1: The three dimensions of agency (see Emirbayer & Mische 1998)

These three analytically distinguished features interweave in concrete action and the authors therefore opt for speaking of a "chordal triad of agency". Not all aspects of these elements relate to world-views in the same way or degree. In the iteration dimension of agency it is mainly the maintenance of expectation that is related to world views, while in the projective element world views are important as they come to bear mainly on its specific mediating place between iteration and practical-evaluative aspects. It includes (especially under modern conditions) a relationship between past experiences and movements towards purposefully and rationally constructed futures. The authors see projectivity as involving "[…] a first step toward reflectivity, as the response of a desirous imagination to problems that cannot satisfactorily be resolved by the taken for granted habits of thought and action that characterise the background structure of the social world" (Emirbayer & Mische 1998: 984). In a similar way, practical evaluation involves posing the problem with respect to specific situations and deliberation as well as decision making, all of them components that relate agency directly with world views, as they involve human capacity for reasoning and making choices.

Lacking the space and time for a more profound exposition of the complex details of this relationship, I would like to make a brief intermediate summary. Agency may be seen as being influenced by world views mainly on the two dimensions of projectivity and of practical evaluation, because both of them are affected by the concrete patterns of a specific world view in so far as these patterns function as selectors for trajectories of action that the actors involved may perceive as possible, choose or try to attain. All these aspects can be investigated in empirical sociological research, insofar as they affect directly the ability of actors to engage with their structural environments, to respond to perceived variations or to potentially transform them. Of course, that applies mainly to the practical-evaluative dimension, as here concrete indicators can be identified: for instance, temporal improvisation, resistance and contention, local action, public deliberation or (political) decision making. It should be emphasised, moreover, that these interdependencies and reflexive effects of world views and agency are not only intentional, but may also be pre- or sub-intentional in relation to conscious action. Especially with regard to those world views that Weber classified as contemporary and this-worldly oriented, the dominance of inner-worldly and practical-ethical action-orientations frequently entails a general embedding of these reflexive effects in everyday action, and all the interpretations and planning that this necessarily involves tend to become routines. This consideration may be of importance for the arguments that will follow.

The globalisation of world views or the world views of globalisation?

One of the most detrimental interpretations of globalisation is the tendency to equate it with a world-wide diffusion of "Western" modes of thought and normative standards, ways of sociality as well as lines of political reasoning and acting. Such an interpretation is not only misleading, but also highly ideological, as it involves a quasi-perpetuation of the old polarisations that have for so long inspired modernisation concepts and analyses. In this sense, it would well be legitimate to perceive the world-wide diffusion of interpretive and normative standards for practical action and its results that go with the supposedly generalised influence of capitalist economic procedures as a diffusion of the practical inner-worldly oriented ethic that Max Weber had associated with European rational world view and eventually, to speak of a globalisation of a specific world view, or world views, if we are willing to accept that even in its homeland this specific perspective has not gone uncontested. In short, this would amount to a crude "globalisation as homogenisation" thesis, and I think that at the present stage of the general discussion such a perspective is no longer legitimate.[3] If instead we conceive – following Anthony Giddens (1990) – globalisation in a very abstract sense as a form of extreme stretching and compression (Harvey

---

[3] The globalisation debate has undergone different phases and has meanwhile certainly overcome the limitations imposed by the simple initial conceptual reduction to economically and financially induced processes of global interdependence. For sociologically informative orientations on globalisation see: Hannerz 1998, Held, McGrew, Goldblatt and Perraton 1999, Held & McGrew 2000, Urry 2003.

1989) of time-space relationships, then we win considerable space for analytical precision. Foremost, it becomes possible to see globalisation as a series of time-space processes by which not only different world views are brought into a relationship to one another, but these different world views also refer ever more frequently and explicitly to globalisation (in the denoted abstract sense) as the pivotal normative and interpretative background for present meanings and as the axis to project futures. The interweaving and the mutual interpenetration, the growing consciousness of past and present interdependencies and the necessary emphasis on distinctive features of different world views is the real activating influence that globalisation exerts on so many world views. Beyond the evidently fetishistic dimension[4] that characterises many arguments about the consequences of globalisation, sociologists may find some relief in a variation of the Thomas' theorem: if people think that globalisation is real, it is real in its consequences. One of these consequences concerns world views and I think it is therefore much more informative to speak of world views of globalisation, than of globalisation of (specific, dominant) world views. In this sense, "globalisation" is an experience that many African or Latin American peoples have made very consciously long before (for instance) European peoples in their majority have perceived it as a real influence in their lives (Randeria 1999). So, when speaking about the relationships of globalisation, world views and agency it must be borne in mind that precisely this same appreciation is also relevant for the empirical dimensions of agency: iterative, practical and projective dimensions of agency are in a similar way profoundly affected by globalisation. Of course not only as an abstract quality, but in concrete ways, as some features of the time-space-stretch/compression that is at the hard core of globalisation, have taken the form of specific (historical) patterns of interpretation of norms and action that also influence the world views of globalisation.

The changed situational logic of development

It is to these patterns that the CfP of this Conference makes reference, when it argues that "world views are expressed in notions of human rights, democracy, neoliberalism, political domination or claims of interpretive hegemony". All

[4] The Oxford Dictionary explains the noun "fetish" as: "an inanimate object worshipped for its supposed magical powers or because it is considered to be inhabited by a spirit".

these categories are focal points of globalisation, because for instance democracy or human rights are not univocal categories, but should be interpreted as frameworks of and for agency which has to operate on them under the criteria of their global interconnectedness. This involves of course a shift in the patterns which are considered to be part of such frameworks: not all options of action are acceptable. As they involve the perception and definition of the situation of action from the point of view of the actors, they constitute a specific logic of the situation. Thus, a process of pre-selection is set in motion that functions across the world views of globalisation. These selective processes become most evident in the real testing ground of practical action. There they are observable in the situational logic that the collective, corporate or individual actors apply and come to experience themselves in the interpretation of the circumstances in which they operate.[5] A case in point is a social situation that is defined by the actors involved as a "development situation". Such situations are typical constellations defined by the world views of globalisation. Not only the classification of countries, of regions, of villages or social collectives as "in need of development" presupposes such an interrelation, as can be observed for instance in the global category of the "Human Development Index".[6] It serves in the first place, as basis for relative measurement, but its components also indicate new patterns in the framework of agency. As a relative quality or a process designating the status or the needs of a specific collective, "development" has been replaced in the meantime by criteria that – in the words of Jan Nederveen Pieterse (2000: 136) – imply new differences: "…(D)evelopmental globalism has become the successor to developmentalism; structural adjustment has become the successor to modernization (…). (D)evelopment policy has increasingly come to mean world market integration (…). If development was traditionally premised on the principle of a special status and treatment of developing countries, globalization means the end of development". Where these criteria prevail, there the performance of single actors under market conditions and in an interaction

---

[5] Following the indications of Michael Schmid (2006: 120, fn. 839) it can be assumed that where there are good reasons to do so, a unified intention and an "institutional use function" (Voss 1985: 93) can be ascribed to corporate or collective actors (for instance, firms, organisations, public agencies, etc.), so that the difference to individual actors may be neglected in this context.

[6] As a standard for global comparison the HDI is explicitly a category intended for a globalising project.

order of competition is the most important measure. This is also latently effective in such categories as human rights, democracy or even "neoliberalism" (even when this category may be more precisely seen as a name for a political programme and an ideology) – all of them refer to the potential of agency of single actors and the postulate of its universality is a normative pattern. As a result, these new patterns that have become part of the world views of globalisation necessarily imply a new situational logic and may open up other possibilities for the analysis of the interrelationship of world views and agency.

The uses of the social mechanism-concept in an actor-oriented development sociology

The generalisation of these criteria by submitting the logic of the situation as defined by the world views of globalisation to the market performance of single actors implies that these criteria are not restricted only to intentional action, but that as pre- or sub-intentional meanings they also permeate the interpretation of many everyday situations. Searching for a concept that permits us to interpret and to explain actor constellations under the premises of agency framed by the specific situational logic of globalisation, it may be therefore helpful to take a look at a sociological discourse that recently has paid great attention to its conceptual stringency and the attainment of explanatory potential – the concept of social mechanisms (see Hedström & Swedberg 1998). This concept has one definite aim: it is oriented to the explanation of social facts or processes in generalised social actor constellations and is not restricted to specific situations. Of course, not all explanations can be based on the workings of such mechanisms and only some social situations may be explained in this way. But I would like to introduce into my argument as a working hypothesis the idea that under the conditions of generalised world-views that refer themselves to globalisation and that are incorporated in the constitution of agency, the explanation by social mechanisms may be a more helpful instrument than it has been before, as its argument focuses on action theory and submits its explanation to the strategic rules of methodological individualism. The following considerations are therefore based on the recent suggestions of Andrea Maurer (2006) and Andrea Maurer and Michael Schmid (2007).

The best known structural-individualistic model of sociological explanation is based on a simple theory of rational choice, as it has been used for instance by James S. Coleman.[7] This has been modified in the meantime, so that it now also incorporates norm-oriented or interpretive action as rational orientations and can function as a multi-level-explanation.[8] Consequently, the many critiques that have been formerly levied against the limitations of the implicit rational choice model have also caused important reorientations of the mechanism approach.[9] The explanatory model starts, firstly, with the determination of the action situation from the point of view of the actors and the alternatives of action that are of relevance for the explanatory problem (situational logic). The presuppositions of social action (resources of the actors such as knowledge, capabilities, etc.) allow for an ordering of the alternatives and their evaluation, so that the action identified as rational for this situation can be explained. Then, the actions that have been explained are combined to social effects by the application of rules of transformation. By this means relevant and interrelated situations of social interdependence (for instance, problems of coordination or of distribution) can be modelled as typical/problematic interdependencies and applied to individual action in very different contexts. The application of rules of transformation (for instance, step-by-step models or threshold models) allows us to comprehend the situative social interdependencies of action. In this way, individual actions can be translated into collective or macro effects of action.[10] Such explanations establish a dynamic relationship between the original situation, the processes of action and their effects, and the necessary conditions of social process. A mechanismic explanation additionally recurs to typical reflexive backward effects that as a consequence of aggregated action for their part influence further action, so that a typical social process gets started that brings about specific distribution patterns. Mechanismic explanations therefore differ from simple step-by-step explanations in that they identify such an explicit recursive function that establishes a dynamic relationship between the actions of the actors and systematic variations of the situation. Such recursive functions can be models of segregation, of accumulation or of dif-fusion that translate situational

7 See Coleman 1990 and the commentaries in Mayntz 2003.

8 Cf. the discussion in Woods 2001.

9 See Maurer 2006: 152, Coleman & Fararo 1991.

10 See Maurer & Schmid 2006: 5 ff.

factors into action and this for its part again into typical variations of situational factors and so on. Consequently, to be useful as an explanatory device, the concept of social mechanism needs an explicit reflexive turn[11] that establishes a dynamic function by the relationship between the action of the actors and the systematic change of the situation. The reflexive turn also presupposes an important feature that has already been important in the analysis of agency: the dimension of time. It is precisely this time axis along which the social mechanism functions. To the degree that the concept of social mechanism aims at the explanation of systematic interdependencies at an intermediate level, then, I think it could be useful for the explanation of some situations that have been deeply affected by the influence of globalisation processes (their "world views"). That could be especially the case with the formation of specific frameworks within these world views, because as a consequence they imply a new situational logic and this logic then becomes part of the constitutive dimensions of agency.

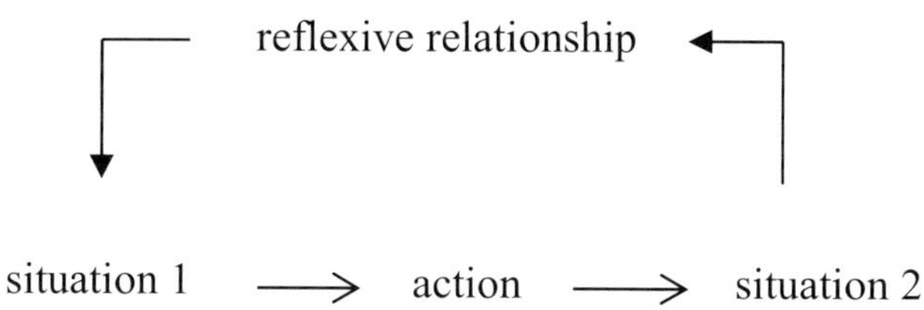

Fig. 2: The logic of a social mechanism explanation

Changing world views as selectors of situational logic

I have already suggested, following Jan Nederveen Pieterse, that the social situation of "development" has been deeply modified by globalisation in the sense that it is being systematically interpreted as integration or at least capacity for integration in market processes.[12] Besides its evident economically reductionist

---

[11] See Maurer 2006: 153; Maurer & Schmid 2007: 5-7. In Schmitt, Florian and Hillebrandt (eds.) (2006) the modelling of reflexive social mechanisms is discussed in detail.

[12] A similar argument is presented in the Editorial of the review "Peripherie" 103 (2007), that observes precisely about the category of "success": "Das verbindet Erfolg mit Entwicklung, die ebenfalls anhand von bestimmten Parametern gemessen wird, welche letztlich einem Konsens darüber entspringen, was Entwicklung sei. [...] Entwicklung meint unter diesem Vorzei-

meaning it is permeated by a single actor logic that functions as background for a concept of agency that is predominantly market oriented. One of the most impressing evidences for this shift is the generalised use of the capabilities approach of Amartya Sen (1985, 2002) and its connections with the Human Development Index, that intends to establish a global classificatory systematic according precisely to such a single actor logic and the abstract individual capacity to participate in social spaces that are organised as (world-) markets. This is a good example to illustrate the idea that an important common denominator of the world views of globalisation is precisely their single actor orientation. Beyond any substantivist specification, this is the common ground of "democracy", of "human rights", of neoliberal "structural reforms", etc. Accordingly, situations of "development" in my opinion are one of the constellations to which the social mechanisms approach could be applied for a sociological explanation of specific problematic results that may arise. There is therefore no need to recur to a cultural interpretation by taking reference to values or norms and to seek a clash of values or an incompatibility of culturally defined norms, to explain results of action in development situations that lead to a deterioration of material or social life conditions of specific groups, quasi-groups or individual actors. The norms and values are already integrated in the specific logic of the situation to that agency in the world views of globalisation adapts itself. These world views, consequently, function as selectors, insofar as they recur to a specific turn in the possible range of various interpretations, favouring the single actor agency under the situational logic of development as "market integration".

Explanatory potential and fields of further research

Mechanisms describe typical sequences of action and explain them by the social action of involved actors. The explanatory potential of the social mechanism approach then, resides on its sociological focus toward specific models of typical social situations that can be translated into socially relevant problem situations. Specific situations that from the point of view of typical actors are characterised by certain factors lead to a processual distribution of options for action. Their concrete effects are evaluated by the actors and by this they become caus-

chen die Zurichtung der ‚Entwicklungsländer' auf den OECD-dominierten Weltmarkt" (Editorial Peripherie 103 (2007): 251.

al factors for specific actor preferences. Therefore, as I have indicated before, an explanation of social processes by a social mechanism needs an explicit reflexive function that establishes a dynamic relationship between the action and a systematic change of the situation. Of course, this does not necessarily presuppose that the actors, whose action becomes reflexive by the resulting effects on the social situation, are always able to understand or to act intentionally on the social mechanism in which they are participating. In the case that has been briefly described – the social situation of development under the conditions of a situational logic determined by world views of globalisation – the operating social mechanism can be identified as a specific variant of the power-mechanism[13] in the action field defined by this situation of development. I would like to suggest that this mechanismic procedure can be applied to explain a situation that typically can be identified when different actors are bound up in such a constellation and their participation is conditioned by the idea that their success ("development") is equated with an on-going effort to engage (successfully?) in a competitive ("market") relationship. The social process of constant competition by itself continuously produces situations that are perceived by the actors as precarious, a success that may be revocable anytime, always under the threat that it may lead to a worse situation for them and a relative falling behind in comparison to the other actors involved.[14] Success for one actor therefore, necessarily means failure for the others and in such a sense "development" may become a zero-sum game, where specific strategies to accumulate power and monopolise resources are necessary (see Fig. 3).

[13] See Maurer & Schmid 2007.

[14] See Maurer & Schmid 2007: 9-12 for the explanation of the power mechanism involved in Elias' argument about the competition among the rulers for the monopoly on land in the civilisation process.

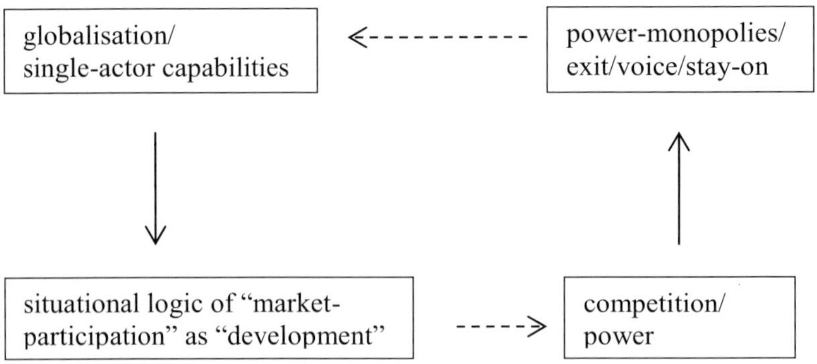

Fig. 3: Social mechanisms in a development situation

This model may be expanded by including aspects already identified by Albert O. Hirschman (1970) and rediscovered for the discussion about the uses of mechanismic analysis in sociology by Andrea Maurer (2006: 154-159). This refers to the two options of action open to actors in an organisation, when they see themselves involved in a process of decreasing functional output of this organisation (or, when applying the idea to the example explained before, they consider the constellation that has crystallised around the specific situation of development to be a downward way for them). They can either leave this situation, redefining their interests and refusing to stay on under worsening conditions in a context of "development", opting therefore for an "exit"-way out (of the market), as Hirschman named this possibility, and seeking another action context that can be interpreted according to other parameters. Or, and that would be the second possibility, they can protest, making their "voice" heard (Hirschman), and can – as a possible option – organise themselves in collective action and stay on in the situational logic of "development" whilst trying to influence the all-encompassing competitive behaviour that underlies the situation through the world views of globalisation. Certainly, it may be considered if there is not a third alternative for the actors involved. As has already been suggested (Maurer 2006: 159), actors could also opt for the possibility to stay on and do nothing, i.e. opting neither for the "exit" nor for the "voice" solution – and that would mean that they also unwittingly reinforce a necessary ideological substrate of globalisation as a process in time: the promise of a diffuse "better world" for the winners, what as a spin-off also generates a result that may be truly invaluable in globalisation: the illusion of hope for a better future.

It may then be a question only to be resolved by research along these lines, whether the social mechanism approach can contribute to a necessary empirical foundation of the effects of world views of globalisation on agency in development situations and by that possibly further an actor-oriented sociology of development.

References

Archer, Margaret (1995): *Realist Social Theory: The Morphogenetic Approach*. Cambridge: Cambridge University Press.

— (1996): *Culture and Agency. The Place of Culture in Social Theory*. Cambridge: Cambridge University Press (rev. Ed.).

Banfield, Edward C. (1958): *The Moral Basis of a Backward Society*. Glencoe: Free Press.

Berger, Peter L. and Thomas Luckmann (1966): *The Social Construction of Reality*. New York: Anchor Books.

Bohman, James (1999): Practical Reason and Cultural Constraint: Agency in Bourdieu's Theory of Practice. In: Shusterman, Richard (ed.): *Bourdieu. A Critical Reader*. Oxford: Blackwell, 129-152.

Bourdieu, Pierre (1977): *Outline of a Theory of Practice* (tr. R. Nice). Cambridge: Cambridge Univ. Press.

— (1990): *The Logic of Practice* (tr. R. Nice) Cambridge: Stanford University Press. (French Original (1980): *Le sens pratique*. Paris: Editions Du Minuit.

Coleman, James S. (1990): *Foundations of Social Theory*. Cambridge: Harvard University Press.

Coleman, James S. and Thomas S. Fararo (eds.) (1991): *Rational Choice Theory: Advocacy and Critique*. Los Angeles: Sage.

Emirbayer, Mustafa and Ann Mische (1998): What Is Agency? *American Journal of Sociology* 103 (4), 962-1023.

Foster, George M. (1979): *Tzintzuntzan: Mexican Peasants in a Changing World*. New York: Elsevier (rev. Ed.).

Giddens, Anthony (1990): *The Consequences of Modernity*. Stanford: Cambridge University Press.

Goetze, Dieter (2006): *Social Theory and Development Sociology at the Crossroads*. Working Paper 356 of the Research Centre Transnationalism and Development Sociology of Bielefeld University: Bielefeld.

Hannerz, Ulf (1998): *Transnational Connections: Culture, People, Places*. London: Routledge.

Harvey, David (1989): *The Condition of Postmodernity*. Oxford: Basil Blackwell.

Hedström, Peter and Richard Swedberg (eds.) (1998): *Social Mechanisms. An Analytical Approach to Social Theory*. Cambridge: Cambridge University Press.

Held, David, Anthony McGrew, David Goldblatt and Jonathan Perraton (1999): *Global Transformations. Politics, Economics and Culture*. Cambridge: Stanford University Press.

Held, David and Anthony McGrew (2000): *The Global Transformations Reader: An Introduction to the Globalization Debate*. Cambridge: Polity Press.

Hirschman, Albert O. (1970): *Exit, Voice and Loyalty*. Cambridge, Mass.: Harvard University Press.

Kalberg, Stephen (2004): The Past and Present Influence of Worldviews. *Journal of Classical Sociology* 4 (2), 139-163.

Maurer, Andrea (2006): Soziale Mechanismen und das strukturindividualistische Erklärungsprogramm. Zur forschungspraktischen Verortung sozialer Mechanismen. In: Schmitt, Marco, Florian Michael and Frank Hillebrandt (eds.): *Reflexive soziale Mechanism*en. Wiesbaden: VS Verlag, 141-164.

Maurer, Andrea and Michael Schmid (2007): *Mechanismen in der erklärenden Soziologie. Zur Logik und Forschungspraxis mechanismischer Erklärungen am Beispiel des Machtmechanismus*. Verhandlungen des 32. Soziologiekongresses in Kassel. Frankfurt and New York: Campus.

Mayntz, Renate (2003): Mechanisms in the Analysis of Social Macro-Phenomena. *Philosophy of the Social Sciences* 34 (2), 237-259.

Nederveen Pieterse, Jan (2000): Globalization North and South. *Theory, Culture & Society* 17 (1), 129-137.

Parsons, Talcott (1968): On Commitments. *Sociological Inquiry* 38, 135-160.

— (1978): *Action Theory and the Human Condition*. New York: Free Press.

Randeria, Shalini (1999): Jenseits von Soziologie und soziokultureller Anthropologie. Zur Ortsbestimmung der nichtwestlichen Welt in einer zukünftigen Sozialtheorie. *Soziale Welt* 50, 373-382.

Schluchter, Wolfgang (1980): *Rationalismus der Weltbeherrschung*. Frankfurt/M.: Suhrkamp.

Schmid, Michael (2006a): *Die Logik mechanismischer Erklärungen*. Wiesbaden: VS Verlag.

— (2006b): Zur Logik mechanismischer Erklärungen in den Sozialwissenschaften. In: Schmitt, Marco, Florian Michael and Frank Hillebrandt (eds.): *Reflexive soziale Mechanismen*. Wiesbaden: VS Verlag, 31-64.

Schmitt, Marco, Florian Michael and Frank Hillebrandt (eds.) (2006): *Reflexive soziale Mechanismen*. Wiesbaden: VS Verlag.

Sen, Amartya (1985): *Commodities and Capabilities*. Amsterdam: North-Holland Publishing.

— (2002): *Rationality and Freedom*. Cambridge: Oxford University Press.

Sewell, William H. (1992): A Theory of Structure: Duality, Agency, and Transformation. *American Journal of Sociology* 98 (1), 1-29.

Tudor, Andrew (1995): Culture, Mass Communication and Social Agency. *Theory, Culture & Society* 12 (1), 81-107.

Urry, John (2005): *Global Complexity*. Cambridge: Polity Press.

Voss, Thomas (1985): *Rationale Akteure und soziale Institutionen. Beitrag zu einer endogenen Theorie des Tausches*. Munich: Oldenburg.

Weber, Max (1920/1972): Zwischenbetrachtung. *Gesammelte Aufsätze zur Religionssoziologie* 1. Tübingen: Mohr, 537-73.

Woods, Philip A. (2001): Values-Intuitive Rational Action: The Dynamic Relationship of Instrumental Rationality and Values Insights as a Form of Social Action. *British Journal of Sociology* 52 (4), 687-706.

Why Things Go Wrong: Agency and Evil among the Kapsiki of North Cameroon

Walter E. A. van Beek

The world is precarious and perilous.
John Dewey[1]

Agency, from freedom to explanation

As one of the new development-oriented concepts, "agency" is used mainly as a corrective on overly structural as well as overly global approaches. Development sociology and anthropology often emphasise the structural factors in development processes, stressing context over creativity, organisation over the individual. Increasingly, against this structural current, the notion of agency surfaces as a counterpoint, reminding planners and analysts that societies and structures consist of people, of individuals, of innovators and of people who give meaning to their lives in specific ways and actors who change their surroundings. This is a useful counterpoint and sorely needed. But it has one corollary: this discourse generates an ideological content in the notion of agency, loading it with emotive content, in fact a positive charge: agency is "good", irrevocably positive. The general image is that of the stubborn individual, battling his limitations, striving for excellence within constraints that are less than "enabling" (Giddens 1990), the little hero who succeeds against overwhelming odds. Characteristic are the analyses of the least-enabled in African societies, such as street children who in studies are either victims of their circumstances – the easiest approach – or full of agency. Thus, agency gives the flavour of success in an uphill battle. Of course, many Africans live in difficult circumstances with limited options for self-determination but they are very creative at the "bricolage" of their own lives. By manoeuvring between his/her social and ideological structures, anyone can create at least some free space for action and meaning for him/herself, which ultimately is inalienably good in any society.

[1] Cited in Reynolds-Whyte 1997: 18.

In this article I divest the notion of agency from its ideological leanings, and explore a different side of it.[2] Agency in social theory[3] involves the dialogue actors engage in with their structured environment, in which on the one hand the actions are informed by the environment and, on the other, by the dynamics of agency itself. Evidently, the very structure that agency acts and reacts on, in itself is only discernible through the interaction of agents with their environment.

So the notion of agency implies an external world that is viewed as external by the agent and has structural features of recognisability and predictability, both for the agent and the analyst. In this external world, the structure has some authority against which the agent is accountable for his actions since acts have consequences and one may be held accountable for them. Of course, that means that some actions are more important than others and that the exercise of agency in some fields is more relevant than in others (Cronk 1999: 49). My point here is that not only "good" is attributed to agency but also "evil", to put it in terms of this slightly essentialist but crucial opposition. Agency is a theory of causation: Alfred Gell (1998: 15) stresses an explanation of "why things happen", not the explanation maybe but a culturally viable one. If an event is attributable to well-known regularities, even laws, it is the environment and not the agent who causes the event. Sunrise is perfectly explainable by general laws without an external agent.[4] So agency is a way of explaining in a particular culture why things which are not evident are as they are. While the major features of society and culture have their own etiological explications, as in myths, the specific happenings and mishaps can and often will be explained by referring to the

---

[2] The concept of "evil" is not very common in anthropological discourse. Stemming from the phenomenology of religion, it was introduced in anthropological debates in the 80s. The assumption is that the notion of evil is applicable outside the Judeo-Christian context from which it entered Western discourse; an opposition between good and evil, defined in whatever form, has been shown to be present in many religions and world views and given the near ubiquity of the opposition, a similar cluster of concepts on "evil" may well be found in most religions (Parkin 1986, van Beek 1994, Mitchell 2001). In this article I refrain from the issue of whether modernisation enhances notions and images of evil (cf. Thoden van Velzen 2001, Meyer 2001, Clough 2001).

[3] The main theoreticians I refer to are Giddens 1990, Archer 1996, Gell 1998, Aronoff 1976 and the seminal article of Emirbayer & Mische 1998.

[4] At least it is in our culture, in contrast to e.g. classic Aztec society where many agents, priests and kings were engaged in complex rituals in order to ensure that the sun rose every morning.

agency of self or third parties. This is true of mishaps in particular and is my point in this contribution.

In times of hardship, people ponder their own agency versus that of others. Gell (1998: 16) calls agency "a culturally prescribed framework for thinking about causation", or in short, "agents cause things to happen".[5] This kind of explanation in ordinary daily life has a background quality that comes to the fore in times of stress, mishap, illness and catastrophe. The temporal dimension is crucial. Mustafa Emirbayer and Ann Mische (1998) stress the projective and iterative elements of agency. Agents review their past actions and those of others, overview their present situation to preview the courses of action towards the future basing themselves on their interpretation of the past, both for their own actions and for those expected of third parties. They expect the world to be predictable and events to more or less repeat themselves, to have some normalcy. So the expectations, hopes, fears and desires of actors vis-à-vis their projected futures are rooted in their evaluation of the past, their assessment of the present and the options they see ahead. And it is exactly at the intersection of past and present that the agency of the third party, the "other", receives full attention. No better or at least no easier explanation exists of "why things go wrong" than interference by an external agent. That can be an impersonal agent, such as fate[6] or a distant one, like the gods, but often is closer – like an ancestor – or within the "gate", such as witches and sorcerers. As explanation of a more general nature, complot theories also work well in explaining misfortune, the agent becoming a featureless "them" which can be filled in according to need. One interesting question then arises: Giddens (1990) uses the notion of "enabling constraints" in his analysis of agency: the structures embedding the agent both limit his options and direct his creative efforts. Can the notion be profitably applied to destructive or harmful agency as well?

"Misfortune happens really": explaining events in Kapsiki

The case I present here is from the Kapsiki and the Higi of North Cameroon and Northeastern Nigeria, an agricultural group living in the Mandara Mountains on

---

5 See Ellis & Ter Haar 2004 for an analysis of power in these terms.

6 As among the Nigerian Tallensi, Fortes 1959 and Horton 1983.

the border between the two countries.[7] If agency is a theory of causation, then what events should be explained? What happenings, in the life of a Kapsiki, are deemed worthy of theoretical thought? My inspiration in this article is an expression used by Kweji Mbeleve, a Kapsiki neighbour of mine, who I met at Cewuve the blacksmith[8] diviner's house. "I always go to Cewuve for the crab [divination] because he tells me what misfortune (*wushi ndrimi*[9]) is going to happen, and misfortune happens really." I encountered this slightly pessimistic outlook in many other conversations: a real happening is something harmful, dangerous or scary. Daily life is OK as long as nothing "happens", and those happenings have to be explained as an infringement of normality. And for those happenings, something or someone is responsible, a cause, i.e. an agent, natural or supernatural. What kinds of misfortune call for an explanation? No indigenous classification is readily at hand, so I will rely on the things people have brought up in conversation and on the problems surfacing through that quintessential monitor of social problems, divination. I will discern four types gleaned from a sample of divination cases.[10]

The first is illness, the second is a setback in plans, a third is an unusual experience and the fourth is general insecurity vis-à-vis an incomprehensible world. These problems give rise to questions of three kinds: who?, how? and why? The first question explores the ways in which misfortune arrives. Is illness generated by an agent? Am I paying for my own mistakes or for the ill-will of someone else? What actions have generated this misfortune? "How" questions

---

[7] The group is called Kapsiki in Cameroon and Higi in Nigeria, and sometimes independently referred to, but in fact must be considered one ethnic group. Research was carried out by the author in 1972-73, with revisits every 4 or 5 years, financed by NWO/WOTRO (Dutch Science Foundation), Utrecht University, the African Studies Centre at Leiden, and several other sources. For ethnographic details, see van Beek (1987, 1994, 1997, 2002, 2007, 2009, 2012b).

[8] I will use the term "smith" for the whole category of specialists the Kapsiki indicate with "rerhè", and "blacksmith" only for those smiths who actually work metal, which happens to be the case with Cewuve. The distinction between smiths and non-smiths is complex, but definitely hierarchical: the smiths are considered the lower echelon, a fundamental distinction for which an olfactorial expression is used, their smell (van Beek 2010).

[9] I use in this article a simplified orthography, in which "rh" indicates a voiced guttural fricative, the "h" a voiceless one, and the "c" a voiceless palatal affricate, like in coa**ch**.

[10] The Nyole discern four types of misfortune: failures of health, prosperity, gender and personal safety (Reynolds-Whyte 1997: 16, 17). These overlap with the categories I found, i.e. illness includes both health and gender failure, setback conforms to failure of prosperity, general insecurity conforms to personal safety; only my 'unusual experience' category is different.

easily spill over into "why" questions, which is crucial in, for example, witchcraft studies. The answer as to "why" informs us of the agent (which can be myself) and moves from mechanism to intent: I want to know how misfortune arrived but if an agent is at stake, the only real and satisfactory explanation is to know the reasons the agent had for his actions. As Reynolds-Whyte (1997: 30) stated for the Nyole: divination moves quickly from the why me? to the why you?, why did you do this to me? i.e. from introspection to extrospection. And it is the latter explanation that is the easiest to understand, usually as the great majority of these reasons are found in everyday life, in daily interaction, in the problems and tensions present in one's immediate surroundings, which – evidently – are well known. Thus, agency as a local theory of causation creates a link between unexpected events with the small-scale processes of social life. Agency reduces the unexpected to the well-known.

Misfortune is the arrival of evil (*ndrimi*) in one's life, an unwelcome but definitely real event. But evil is not something that exists independently of agents (Parkin 1985). On the back of misfortune are bad things, bad people, people with bad intentions or simply bad unintended effects of their or one's own actions. It is also generated by supernatural beings which are not normally evil, but neither always good. The crucial issue is one of ambivalence, of all agents. The notion of agent implies a choice, located in the other, with an intentionality that is not self-evident, that is not predictable but can be understood, as the agent is effectively similar to ourselves. It is this ambivalence, this capriciousness that drives the explanation. The agent is the random factor in social events and it is exactly this agent-generated randomisation of events that gives credence to the explanation.

First and foremost among misfortunes is illness, without any doubt. About half of the divination cases at the smith's are generated by health problems and for the Kapsiki this definitely includes infertility. Actually, infertility is one major issue in divination, as it can be caused by many actions and agents. Thus we explore several divination cases performed with the crab, an animal used extensively in North Cameroonian divination (van Beek 2012a). A smith, an important ritual intermediary in Mandara culture, is usually the main mediator, though sometimes a clairvoyant can do the job as well (see infra). The diviner uses a large pot with sand and water, lined with straws indicating the client, his or her social environment and the problem. The diviner asks the crab a question and then puts it in the pot, where it rearranges a number of calabash shards decorated with different signs. Every fifteen minutes, the smith pulls off the lid and interprets the changes and traces by the crab. A session takes about two hours.

The case of the half-brother

> Zra puts his problem to Cewuve, the blacksmith: "My second wife, Kwaberhe Kwampa, for whom I paid a large bride price, still has no child. She is a good wife, she did not run away in these years but she has no rest, for she has not been pregnant for all these years. We often asked the crab but she is still not pregnant. Could you see what is really the matter?"
>
> Zra is anxious to get some answers from Cewuve, the blacksmith, who knows well what is the matter in Zra's compound and proceeds immediately. With the crab in his hand, the smith explains to the little animal what might be the reason behind the problem: "Kwashukwu seems to be infertile. Is it something her former husband did? Has he 'spoilt' her with magic? Tell me, do not lie." He puts the crab in the wet sands and closes the pot off with the remnants of an old jar. After a quarter of an hour, Cewuve takes off the lid and inspects how the crab has rearranged the loose shards in the wet sand. "Nothing special. Some bad news from the fields of Zra. What is it?" The crab gets a specific suggestion this time: "Kuve and Sunu Ma [Zra's half-brother] and his wife Kuve, maybe they should sow some sorghum in the field, dig it up again, grind it and put it on their jars, to avoid problems?"
>
> The crab's second "answer" is clearer: There is nothing wrong with the wives of Zra, but there is some "noise" with Sunu Ma and his wife Kuve. Again the crab is addressed: "Should Kuve take sorghum, walk on the road, take some sand, grind it and make a sacrifice? And should all women give her some ground peanuts?" While the crab works at it, Cewuve remarks: "If *Shala* (God) wants it, Kwashukwu will be pregnant soon and have a son, but Kuve will get matini (two pregnancies in a row)." The session lasts a few more questions, till the fifth one produces more specific information. Indeed, it is Sunu Ma who has to do something. Zra and his wife the next day followed the crab's instructions. A few months later Kwashukwu showed that she was pregnant, not with a boy but a girl. Zra did not complain. Later, Kwashukwu would have four more children, two boys and two girls. The last one would be born after Zra himself had died.

A very natural and evident agent is at work here, i.e. the half-brother. Born of the same father but to a co-wife, half-bothers cause classic tensions in relations in Kapsiki, and Sunu Ma in question is a problem anyway in the village as he disdains hard work and prefers to party and relax. He is judged a little irresponsible in the village. So pointing the finger at him as the – indirect – cause of the problem at hand is quite credible. Anyway, the problem was solved so the crab's anamnesis must have been right. This, of course, is the classic anthropological explanatory strategy of following the fault lines in society, as an explanation of misfortune: the wayward individual has done it. Characteristically, the "who?" is answered, which gives information on the "why?" but without bothering with the "how?". The very fact of a tenuous relationship and a fragile reputation is sufficient for an explanation, and the exact mechanism of misfortune is not deemed relevant. The problem is not the means but the significance, not the intrusion but the redress of the problem by eliminating or appeasing the deeper cause of the misfortune. What is curious in this case is the rapid transition from diagnosis to the redeeming offerings; one probable reason is that all concerned were familiar with the tensions in the family, the diviner being Zra and Sunu Ma's next-door neighbour.

Photo 1: Cevuwe reads the traces made by the crab

A second example gives a more maligned interpretation of the same problem.

The case of the wrong burial

In Danja's compound, a famous diviner who is not a smith but a clairvoyant, a woman from another village asks why, after the death of her first child, she does not get pregnant again. At first the crab indicates a problem with her father but the second and third openings show another reason. Her first child was buried the wrong way by the smith. He misdirected the small body in posture and cardinal direction, and – according to the crab – not by chance or mishap. He tricked the woman into leaving the burial site for a moment and then performed his foul deed. The solution is to go back to the smith in question, induce him to rebury the child at the very same time of the day that the original burial was done, if possible without giving him anything. As he has tricked[11] her, she should do the same and not give him any money. Before she goes to him, she has to sacrifice a chicken on her mother's sacrificial jar with sorghum from a smith and herself, and a goat's bone and throw this along the road on her way to the smith, if possible at a black ants' nest. Then the smith has to bury the child properly: sitting upright, facing east, both hands on top of its head, imploring God to make his mother pregnant again. After that, the woman will become pregnant again, the crab says.

The agent here is clear: the smith who was in charge of the burial (the burial of a young child is done almost privately) was the evil agent. People can be bad, and the smith is the "close other" in Kapsiki society. Smiths (van Beek 1992) form a separate caste as undertakers, musicians and magical specialists, and easily compensate their lower social status with a reputation of being cunning people, powerful in the religious sphere, though not deemed trustworthy. The fact that the diviner was not a smith might have influenced his interpretation in this direction but smiths share this tendency. The agent here is the "other" within the village.

Mishaps of the second category are often linked to the harvest, jobs or travel. The following example centres on the millet harvest.

[11] Rhwete in Kapsiki is an important concept in their value system. It bears no negative value but indicates cleverness and a redressing of social inequalities (van Beek 1975).

The case of the bad harvest

> Kwarumba Yèngu has come to Cewuve because her largest field did not produce nearly enough millet this year. The surroundings fields were fine but hers was not. And as a widow, she is hard pressed for labour. The crab indicates a few lingering problems in her house – her son does not want to leave the house [he should marry] – but then zooms in on a particular grave that borders the field. There is something wrong with that grave. The final prescription is that Kwarumba Yèngu has to use the calabash at the graveside and to perform a sacrifice linking that grave with a graveyard in the vicinity. But this is a major sacrifice, not the usual small-scale kind. She has to make beer and invite her neighbours, which implies that she also has to kill a goat. The remedy indicates, more than the conversation with the crab, the probable cause: her relationship with her neighbours has to be redressed in the same way the relationship of the single dead with his dead kinsmen in the graveyard has to be restored.

Now for the third category of mishaps, frightening experiences, and the following case was a scary one:

The dog nightmare

> Kweji tells his story: "I dreamt last night. I sat on the public square of my ward and the place was full of dead people; I was the only living one. A huge dog from among the dead wanted to kill me, but I wrestled him to the ground again and again. The last time I picked it up and smashed it on the rocks near the dead people; the dog broke into pieces and I was covered with blood. The dead people encouraged me in my battle against the dog. They had homes there as the sweet potato patches we make. I woke up, told my wife and she advised me to consult the crab. She had also dreamt: her son who was among the Fulbé had come to her, all dressed in white. She asked him what he had brought her but he just answered with a smile. Other youngsters, also in white clothes, asked him for his gown but he refused. They retaliated by saying that they would stop him from going to Mubi [in Nigeria]. His mother came between them, then his father told him the youngsters were just joking. At that point she woke up because her husband called her."

Finally, as an example of the fourth category, there is always the general threat of an unknown world out there.

The fear of revenge

> Gwarda, the chief smith consults his fellow smith Cewuve about a particular problem. A long time ago he killed someone in Sena, a village on the Nigerian side of the border. Now he has heard rumours that the people from that village are planning something against him, and he is worried about the *hwa ta Va*, lightening, (lit. knife of Rain). Anyway, he has to make a trip into a village close to Sena and senses danger. He is especially worried that lightening will strike him as revenge for this killing, as the people of Sena are probably looking for Rain [a divinity in Kapsiki religion] to do so. This killing never has been paid for (van Beek 1987) nor has a counter raid been possible due to the arrival of pax gallica.
> The crab quietens his fears: there is no danger of lightening but there is definitely a threat of illness. To travel safely, a sacrifice is called for, as danger is indeed present. After that, the consultation mainly handles the ways of preventing a mishap, i.e. the right sacrifices to make. Eventually, after some dialogue with the crab, the exact nature of the sacrifice is determined and the threat is averted.

Photo 2: Chief smith Gwarda

The agent here is the generalised "other" as fits the hostile relations between Kapsiki villages. The agent is the traditional enemy who not only is highly credible but also gives a handle on how to counter any threat, as the long history of hostility between villages has generated ample means to cope with it, both in the socio-political and the religious sphere. The danger itself is specified but there is only one possible option. Between enemies there are many more dangers but there is no need to elaborate on these as the client, himself a smith, is well aware of other dangers. Cewuve deems it unnecessary to warn against *beshèngu*, harmful magic, as he would have done to someone else; after all, Gwarda is even more of a specialist in this than Cewuve, so they do not discuss the main threat at all, leaving it as self-evident. Gwarda did go, carrying his defences against beshèngu, and returned safely. The world "out there" is still close to home in this example but similar consultations are done on kinsmen in the big cities, and on travel.

The agents

The Kapsiki face misfortune from different angles, in the first instance from family, in the second from a deceitful smith, in the third and fourth from death and the "other world" in number five. To assess these stories, we will consider the various agents in Kapsiki culture that are deemed to be responsible for the afflictions that flesh is heir to. In discerning types of agents, we run through the examples and view their definition of the malign influences impinging on individual lives.

The first and most obvious agent thwarting one's own intentions is the close other. Kapsiki society is not a harmony-oriented culture in which competition and rivalry remain hidden from the roving eye, but more an arena of social relations, some harmonious but the majority not, some with parallel interests but most not. The relationship between half-brothers is paradigmatic: sharing the same father but with different mothers, they lack the close emotional bond that in Kapsiki culture comes through matrilateral links, while they compete for position, inheritance and wealth. According to René Girard (1980), they are each other's model and obstacle, resulting in a precarious balance between bonding and strife. Though misfortune, say evil, can come from outsiders as well, it is more potent when it comes from the inside: if the one who should be benign is in fact fiendish, who is one's ally? For instance, as the closest relative is one's mother, any ill wish from the mother outweighs anything else: Kapsiki curses (*bedla*) can be spoken by anyone but only have to be thought by close kin on the mother's side to be effective. The notion of one's own guilt (fete) is crucial. When a close kinsman/woman does not show proper respect for a mother's brother, the latter may resort to a formal curse. This does not imply a great deal of ritual but is simply spoken: "If so-and-so has misbehaved against me in that manner, then …" A wide variety of afflictions can be administered in this way and the closer the relationship between the parties, the more dangerous the curse, with the most feared curses coming from the mother and her brother. They indeed just have to think of the curse. As the formula indicates, the curse is only effective in cases of factual and serious misbehaviour. It can be eradicated by a simple ritual of blessing but only ex post facto.

The second type of agent is "the institutional other". In our example, this was a smith who is the paradigmatic other. Smiths (rerhè) are a special category of people among the Kapsiki who perform the main ritual functions in society (van Beek 1992): they are not only the village metal workers (for both iron and brass) but also the undertakers; they make music, are well versed in traditional medicine/magic and they perform divination in its various forms. Though not exclusively theirs, most techniques of divination are firmly tied to their craft.[12] This minority (about 5%) is strictly endogamous and the various smith families have links of fictive kinship with the patriclans that make up the fabric of social life in a Kapsiki village. Smiths have the reputation of cunning, of seeing hidden things and of having links with the spirit world. And theirs is the authority to foretell the future and explain the past.

As the non-smith Kapsiki (*melimu*) are more or less their patrons and in any case form the mainstream of society (smith families are attached to various melimu clans), the interests of smiths and melimu run parallel to a fair extent. The well-being of the whole village is paramount but many fault lines run through the village, and the *melimu-rerhè* line is perpendicular to all of these. Thus, a smith can always benefit from both the benevolence of the melimu and their internal strife. A comparison with Western lawyers might be apposite here albeit not in the legal sphere[13] but in the religious one. They are the mediators par excellence with the marginality and lingering suspicion attached to that position.

This inherent danger from one's fellow villager is increased when the other is not simply a competitor but the bearer of real evil. The most harmful people are those who practise beshèngu (black magic). Characteristically they are considered not to be smiths but fellow melimu. As the epitome of evil in Kapsiki

---

12 So the term "smith", though common in the literature on West Africa, is not overly apt, as they are the 'general specialists' among the Kapsiki, as they are among most of the groups in the Mandara region.

13 Legally smiths are considered as children, see van Beek 1987.

society, this magic is practised by someone who aims to harm others by killing them or making them infertile. It is evil because it harms and because it intrudes. The term beshèngu denotes not a specific object or combination of things but a number of different ways of harming other people. Some of those are well known (e.g. the whiskers of the leopard), others are secret and known only to the specialist. Beshèngu is a specialist's job, done professionally by smiths, the ritual intermediaries in Kapsiki culture. Ways to make beshèngu are given by the Kapsiki but in the most general terms because everybody emphatically wants to disclaim having any such knowledge. Fascination centres on the distribution of the material: sorcerers are reputed to train flies to transport beshèngu to their victims, bury it in footpaths, or change themselves into flying creatures to administer their wares. The Kapsiki are sure that all important men have such beshèngu that they have bought from a specialist in another village. However, it is not the possession of beshèngu that is evil in itself but its use. One can defend oneself against possible attack and some kinds are used for protection. In ritual texts and public discussions, curses are formulated against the users. Anyone who walks about with beshèngu (i.e. who carries it with him in order to use it), may drop dead in his tracks. Still, according to some informants, those curses are often mouthed by the very people who own the stuff. The threat of use does not come from inside the compound, such as witchcraft. People think of this kind of sorcery as coming from outside, though never far away.

Beshèngu is, according to the Kapsiki, sought after by people who are kinsmen, probably agnates, who are jealous of their clan and lineage brothers or interested in their misfortune. A large inheritance may trigger the use or accusations of beshèngu, usually between the agnates competing for the inheritance. Treating the resulting illness is difficult and must be done by the same type of specialist who performs the harmful magic. These rites are very secret. Information available on this protection indicates that the content of the rites is highly idiosyncratic, varying from specialist to specialist.

Protection against beshèngu is more important than treatment, and constitutes an important focus of daily religion for the Kapsiki. A person must live carefully, especially if one has social prominence, to minimise any possible dangers. Protection against this threat, which is difficult to realise, focuses on protection against infection, on how to keep "trained" flies away and protect the compound from flying creatures. Constant vigilance is needed and any protection against beshèngu must be kept in good shape. As with all acts aimed at the supernatural, the use of beshèngu carries a risk, as any powerful means can turn against its owner if he is not very careful.

Our third example offers a venue in another type of agent to be feared, less mundane, more of the "other world". The dead are the issue here, their relationship among each other and with the living. Kapsiki religion is not an ancestral religion (van Beek 2007) due to the direct link that everybody has to his or her personal shala, the dead part of the "other side of the world". Elsewhere (van Beek 2012b) I have compared the Kapsiki notion of the other world to the two sides of a paper: the one cannot exist without the other, and one can only see one side at a time. Only those who are removed from that paper can see that there are two sides, having glimpses of both sides at the same time. The relationship with this world is characterised by the ambivalence that pervades the "other side of the world", an ambivalence that is no stranger in the mundane world either for that matter. The general notion is that of *ndegema*, a lack of harmony, or being out of sync, and most often it is shala, the general term for one's personal god, with whom one is in disharmony. "Why" is what divination has to establish. A missed harvest is a serious indi-cator but general malaise or other vague mishaps or feeling thwarted in life are signs as well.

The notion of fete, a mistake, is important, too. Misfortune strikes when the other world has a real claim, a legitimate complaint, so the victim will have to go back deep into his own past to find the problems he might have generated in his recent past, using as many kinds of divination as possible. When an untimely death occurs, people may suspect a sorcerer, in which case the *wuta* ritual is performed, a complicated affair that takes one of the relatives of the deceased to a village far away. The culprit is symbolically killed in a large pot (wuta). Afterwards the relative lets the village know that he has gone to wuta and is waiting for the culprit to die, implying that any future death is a result of this ritual.

The epidemic nature of death by revenge, or death due to one's own fete (fault) is central in another ritual, the *sekwa*. In principle, sekwa is a means of ensuring the repayment of debts: when someone refuses to repay a debt, a creditor may put his sekwa in the debtor's compound and death will strike that compound like an epidemic, wiping out the debtor's household as well as anyone else who has ever eaten there. This sekwa is often used as a threat which is seldom carried out. It is considered a perfectly legitimate means of enforcing repayment, and neither its manufacture nor its possession or use bears any social stigma. Sekwa consists of a bundle of objects; its composition is well known to everyone. There is no remedy against its use except paying the debts immediately. When applied, it is put in the middle of the courtyard, visible to everyone. But things rarely go that far.

Our fourth example moves into eerie experiences, sights of the specifics of the other world, with all the concomitant dangers of that imagined reality. Dogs are a common symbol of spirits and especially death, and thus also of people who dwell in that domain. This is the realm of "different" people, of those people in one's immediate surroundings who have the capabilities to harm. Three types of agents can be discerned. First, there are people who have a bad or special *mehele* (character or spirit). Witches (*mete*) are the clearest example. A witch is someone (male or female) who inherits a special type of *shinangkwe* (shadow) at night and leaves the sleeping body through the anus and roams in the bush, red like fire, as a kind of wild cat. It eats the shadows of sleeping children's hearts. When they wake up, the victims feel weak and become ill. Unless the mete drops the shadow, the victim will die. Witchcraft is considered to inherit matrilineally (in a strictly patrilineal kinship system). The Kapsiki on the whole are well aware of who are mete. Most witches, however, are not "active" but can become so when hit by jealousy, ire or lust for vengeance, which are considered the motor that sets the involuntary processes of witchcraft in motion. So witches are more or less responsible for their vile acts; it is their fete (fault).

However, not every witch is known as such. One major risk for a village lies in strangers coming in and who, because of virilocal residence, tend to be women. Women from outside who marry village men are hardly known at all, so there is the danger of witches being among them. This is probably one reason why women are deemed to be witches more often than men. Many folktales warn young men of the dangers of a beautiful but unknown wife coming into the village after marriage. Kapsiki divination may indicate that a certain illness is the result of mete activities but cannot show who has been active. The high-status diviners known elsewhere in Africa are not found in this area, which ties in with the acephalous juro-political organisation of the Kapsiki, where pronouncing a judgment over others is difficult. The usual reaction after the crab has indicated witchcraft is to cry into the dark of the night: "Let go, let the heart go." Hopefully, the witch will then fear detection and return the shadow of the heart.

It is essential that the mete in question be someone close, either a kinsmen, a wife or co-wife. Witchcraft, as is nearly always the case in Africa, is the "enemy within the gates". If someone, either a known witch or a newly arrived wife, is suspected of taking the shadow of a child's heart, the sick child is put before her in the presence of as many people as possible, saying: "Here it is. Do eat the rest now." In the past, if the child died, the witch was chased out of the village and her ears were cut off. Since colonial days, however, the government has not allowed this and the number of witches has proliferated, people say. In recent years, accusations of witchcraft have regained acceptance in the Cameroonian courts. This has not led to a flood of accusations among the Kapsiki, however, as the main reaction is still "How can anyone else see her eating that heart?" Treatment of mete infliction may be limited but protection is normally easy to obtain. Everybody knows protective medicine and each smith can provide the *rhwè* (medicine) needed for a newborn baby. Kapsiki society is not a witch-ridden society: the number of accusations is small and relatively few illnesses are attributed to witches. Children are deemed to be about the only possible victims of mete, and among children's plights only the combination of diarrhoea without blood, fever and frequent urinating (more or less the symptoms of bacterial dysentery) point to mete influence.

Other harmful people are the men or women with the *hweteru* (evil eye). Their spirits roam the village at night in no specified form and suck blood from people and animals. These victims do not die but become weak and unproductive. These hweteru act out of sheer spite and jealousy, and are deemed to be in command of their bad shadow, which is inherited matrilineally. In this case, people generally do not know who is hweteru in the village. There is no known cure, only protection against them but that is easy to obtain from a common plant species that gives fair protection. However, it is important not to foster jealousy: anything beautiful or enticing must be hidden from view.

A third kind of special people, though much less harmful, are the *kelèngu*, (spirit walkers). It is this type that was dubbed "clairvoyant" above. Their shadows leave them at night in their own image and join colleagues in the village. These shadows are believed to go on noble exploits together like stealing sorghum from enemy fields or waging war against the spirit walkers of neighbouring villages. When they steal the shadow of the harvest, they put it with their own crops; and as a result their supply of grain seems interminable. Their main thrust is against other villages, so people do not consider the kelèngu as shameful or evil and speak freely about it. This characteristic is passed down from father to only one son, and the spirit walkers can be recognised by their thin linear somatic type. They explain their own thinness by their overdose of activity: "We are never at rest; we work during the day and steal at night." As protection, one has to shield fields from the kelèngu of other villages. Some medicinal plants offer this protection, as does a thorn hedge or a row of a black sorghum variety around the field. The kelèngu are sometimes aware of future events, in which case their authority is uncontested, which is one reason they are sometimes dubbed "clairvoyants" in the literature. Whatever they see happening in the spirit world will happen shortly in everyday life. If they kill people among themselves in their battles, that spirit walker will die within a few days. No medicine will help. Women may be walkers too, for any war has to have its spectators.

Our final example is of the chief smith who feared a revenge killing, and having been responsible for the first death he did indeed have good reason to fear for his life. The threat however remained vague, stemming not from sorcery (which is ineffective against a chief smith) but from the beings of the other world: Shala, Rain or Death. The notion of shala implies one's personal god: each person has his shala, "up there", his "double" in the other world. But just as people are related, so are the various shala, eventually merging into one shala pelè rheme, shala in heaven. The notion has many meanings as well: it can imply a place, a mythical snake or a certain kind of illness, all closely associated with God (van Beek 2012b). As usual in African religion, the main supernatural being is ethically neutral because no evaluations are ever made of the events that are deemed to be his work. *Shala menete* (God has done it) is a standard phrase of resignation.

The Kapsiki are confident that ultimately their interest and that of their shala will run parallel but one can never be sure of shala's positive influence at any one time. Even more ambivalent is the relationship between an individual and someone else's shala. The Kapsiki with their individualistic orientation consider the well-being of the one as a threat to another person. An individual can fall out of grace with his/her personal god in many ways, such as the infringement of a taboo. A number of actions are taboo, ranging from forbidden sexual relations to slaughtering a pregnant goat or having a cock crow on one's granary. Not all can be prevented but they still call for reparation or else several kinds of bad things can happen: illness, infertility (as in our example), bad luck in trading or in cultivation. No specific threat is associated with shala-related problems. Protection as such is not possible so careful living is called for and if mishaps occur, divination should indicate the source of the trouble.[14]

Shala-related beings may be dangerous, too; *Va*, the personification of the rain we saw feared for his lightening but also *veci*, the sun, can be encountered in person, which calls for a sacrifice. These beings are relevant in very special situations only, like drought, and then are dealt with collectively, either in a rain sacrifice or in communal rituals. Other dangers lurk in the other side of the world and are even more dangerous. *Mte*, death and some illnesses (measles and smallpox) are conceived as beings, against whom virtually no protective medicine exists. Some specialists claim medicine against smallpox[15] or measles, but no one can resist Mte. In fact, the mythic fight by the cultural hero of the Kapsiki, *Hwempetla* (or *Nayekwakedè*) against Mte and the failure of his many ruses to escape death form the backbone of Kapsiki mythology. As the people of old tried to escape or conquer in vain, no contemporary Kapsiki can hope to postpone death. So against these three there is no real protection, only acceptance.

Of course, some illnesses stem not from personal beings but from epidemics, which are not personified, like malaria, meningitis or dysentery. Against these, there are various rhwè, some well known, others the secret knowledge of the specialists (smiths). Sometimes female infertility is considered among such epidemics but it more often has other causes. Usually the symptoms are clear and well known, and do not call for divination, nor for any kind of personalised agency. Second, the many ways in which rhwè and other special objects that are ritually important can attack people are considered a threat from beyond. Sekwa

---

[14] Here Kapsiki religion diverts from the more ancestor-oriented religions in many other parts of Africa. Shala has so many layers of meaning that the typical negotiation aspect that is so clearly present in, e.g. Nyole divination (Reynolds-Whyte 1997: 31) is less prevalent here. Shala always carries as an overtone the notions of a supreme being, not just a spiritual being, which would be more amenable to negotiation.

[15] The fact of eradication of smallpox has not yet entered Kapsiki consciousness.

is a special case. These objects, like Neolithic remains of former populations, may be used in a variety of ways for the well-being of the owner. All of them, however, may present some danger to the owners. In Kapsiki, no blessing is ever free; what one gains in a special way beyond the average situation will have to be paid for elsewhere and usually these blessings shorten one's lifespan. As no specific kinds of misfortune are attributed to them, they are almost never mentioned in divination.

Between detection and diagnosis: the human side of agency

The reaction to all these inherently or potentially dangerous agents is as varied as the agents themselves. Healing illness is a complicated process, the details of which fall beyond the scope of this chapter (van Beek 2009, 2011), and entails an array of treatments, ranging from folk medicine known by everyone to specialist treatments. If persistent, an illness also demands an on-going process of delving ever deeper into one's history, by accruing ever more divinatory insights. Here I want to dwell on the Kapsiki notion of agency itself, in its meeting with agency of the "other" in its various forms, from ambivalent to evil.

Divination is a kind of detection. In a detective novel the crime is clear, i.e. the problem is a mishap, say someone is dead. Now three questions are posed: how was the victim killed?, who did it? and why? The method of killing gives a clue to the culprit (in detective series the "perp") who has to have the means, was present at the scene and finally has a motive, the "why". Presence and the murder weapon together imply the "how". So the "how" leads to the "who" and then the "why" has to be constructed or found. The logical chain can be interrupted by an absent murder weapon (or body!) but that is solved in many series by the very popular pathologist (or forensic anthropologist!), or by the impossibility of the suspect having been at the crime scene: the alibi (that then should be undermined by the brilliant detective). Finally, when the suspect is almost a culprit, the question of motive has to be answered. The guiding principle is that people do not kill haphazardly or at random but for a reason: they should accrue some benefit from the crime, and with a crime like murder the motive should match the severity of the deed. That motive should be understandable. As outsiders – the detective, the judge and the jury if need be and surely the audience – should be able to feel some empathy towards the motive: they have to be able to imagine themselves in that position and at least considering murder. The motive is the clinching argument, the final reasoning. Often, both in a novel and a TV series, the motive remains hidden till the end and only becomes clear when the real past or real identity of the main players emerges from the mists of the past. Unravelling that past, the detective finds their main and compelling reasons for the act in various ways: they are someone else than they seem to be, they have had past relations with the victim that were well hidden from the curious eye, or they have other convincing skeletons in their cupboard. Once the audience knows who the suspects really are and how they are related, the puzzle is solved. What remains is the final confession, the mistake in the interrogation, the final confrontation with their past or their entrapment in a small but clever scam that reveals their dirty linen.

With serial killers, who are very popular in series these days, it is the motive that becomes the main obsession and the principal puzzle, as serial killers usually have no previous relationship with the victim prior to the murder, and if they do they are well hidden. The detectives – in this case almost always a team – zoom in on their psyche. Serial murders are recognisable by a common "how", their MO (modus operandi), and they derive their identity as a killer from specificities of the gruesome act: they advertise themselves. To some extent, at least. The detectives have two problems. First, the team must clearly identify which murders belong together, and second they must construct a profile of the killer: given the "how" they must construct a theory on the "why". Only then can they either trace his whereabouts through the profile or – and this is the most desirable outcome – predict when he (most serial killers are male in such series) will strike again and catch him red-handed, if possible with a heart-stopping scene in which the main hero almost dies.

How does divination compare with this picture of Western police work? Of course, books and TV series are not overly realistic, as the great majority of murders happen between close kin and are nowhere near as complex or elaborate as in novels or series. But the comparison is apt anyway. Divination digs into the past – and is very reticent about the future – first of all. The problem to be solved is a misfortune that has been caused by someone, an agent/actor. What agent is the culprit is to be found through a perusal of the client's past: human, non-human, own mistake (fete!), or plain evil.

What is unimportant in divination is the "how", for the means by which misfortune is brought, induced or sent to the client is almost never mentioned. If one is ndegema with shala, it is self-evident that shala can send misfortune, in any form. If a witch is the culprit, there is of course a theory as to how she can inflict harm but in what way in the specific case at hand is not interesting and the specifics of beshèngu are only of academic interest (for the anthropologist!). It is the why that divination zooms in on, the reasons behind the affliction, and the motives of the culprit agent. These "why" answers should address two things: how the culprit is in a position to do harm (though exactly how is not important), i.e. what leverage he has over the client. This can be power, previous relations or the guilt of the client. Second, why is the client – the victim – now vulnerable? The motive is usually quite general but the divination has to give some clue to timing and surely to the client's openness for attack.

So the differences in divination are threefold. First, the mechanical, methodological question is ignored: how the agent "did it" is not considered interesting. A general religious theory suffices to bridge the gap between the suspect and the effect of his intentions: the curse of the kinsman, the sekwa with its immediate retribution and shala with his influence. Only when the action swings to the evil pole of societal ethics is the theory more specific, at least there is a more detailed cultural understanding of the processes involved: the witch with his/her sucking of blood, the evil eye with its staring, the sorcerer with his trained flies. The second element is erasing doubt, the notion of proof. The finding mechanism, divination, does not lead to proof but is in itself incipient proof. Incipient as the Kapsiki are always aware of the notion of trust involved in divination: One has to trust the diviner, one has to follow his advice. At least, one has to try out what he recommends. Kapsiki religion – like African religions in general – are about pragmatics and not about creating systems of timeless understanding, instead they focus on hope and intention and not on the production of certainty (Reynolds-Whyte 1997: 24).[16] The proof is in the eating: if the prescriptions of the diviner pan out, if the problems disappear after the recommended sacrifices, then he was right. If not, then another diviner or possibly another system of divination is used, and it is for this reason that most Afri-

[16] "We see people as actors trying to alleviate suffering rather than as spectators applying cultural, ritual, or religious truths." (Reynolds-Whyte 1997: 20).

can cultures have more than one divination system. Divination is done in the shadow of uncertainty and doubt. But any verification will have to be done by a similar process, looking into the past, prescribing ways to solve the problem and engage the future, so the uncertainty remains.

The third element of difference, finally, is that divination adds one element to the detection chain: it has to indicate what measures to take to undo the misfortune, pre-empt another attempt by the culprit, and/or repair the damage. Divination tries to solve the problem, not just the puzzle, and then is not only the detective but also the judge and the jury.

A second comparison comes in with these two latter aspects, i.e. with the process of healing. As shown especially in the first example, the diviner goes quickly to remedy the problem. Diagnosing the patient's problem is the first step, leading to a probable cause of the affliction. Then the physician prescribes a cure to fight the illness. In diagnosis, like in detection, one starts with the anamnesis, the assessment of the patient's medical history. Way of life, experience and exposure to infection hearths are then matched with specific and general clues to formulate a theory of affliction: the detection phase of the healing process is called diagnosis. Following this, a cure is prescribed which has to be applied by the patient. The proof of the theory lies in the future, just as with divination and sacrifice: if the affliction is cured, the diagnosis was correct. If not, a second opinion, as in divination, is called for and both the anamnesis and the tests in the present state are intensified to arrive at a new and better diagnosis. Of course, there are other major differences in the tests themselves, in the reliability and especially the testability of these diagnostic techniques but the logical structure of divination comes to the fore in this comparison.

So, detection plus cure is divination's closest kin, its homologue in the realm of Western science. This brings in another view on agency in Western society, as not only the homology is clear but also the difference in the concept of the agent. In medical detection, the agent is very small, a virus or microbe undetectable to the naked (human) eye is in principle hidden and hard to trace, often only being traceable by its effects. Misfortune leads to the detection of agents, of the "other"; in medicine the ultimate "other" is the smallest possible form of life, a piece of nature that lives and hides inside us and eats us from the inside. It is very much the enemy within the gates, within the gates of the body. It is simply a part of us that should not be there. That medical history shows that this enemy evolved together with both the physical and the social evolution of mankind makes this relationship all the more ironic. This means that in Western society the agency of the ultimate other has been emptied of intent, of motive and of "free will and agency". Thus divination stands between detection and diagnostics: it combines the wilfulness of the culprit with the invisibility of the medical "other".

Now it is time for an answer to the question in the introduction whether Giddens's notion of "enabling constraints" applied to evil agency as well. We have seen that for the Kapsiki the agents of misfortune are manifold and varied, ranging from one's own mistakes, one's own shala to evil outsiders, and from the figure of Death roving the mountains to infectious diseases. Enabling constraints are the background reason for a predictability of actions, in this case of misfortune. And indeed, misfortune for the Kapsiki comes in recognisable, somewhat predictable forms, which means that the evil agents are not considered to have completely free actions: their harmful influences follow defined cultural pathways and their arrival is accompanied by a sign of recognition. A witch can do certain things, not everything, and a sorcerer can train flies for beshèngu transportation, but not grasshoppers. In short, misfortune is kin, evil is family.

This brings us to the final considerations of the notions of causation in Kapsiki, their emic theory of agency. As shown through the divination process and applied to practical problems, notions of agency are ways of signification, logical pathways to give meaning to events, especially to mishaps, mistakes and misfortune. The bleak side of agency that has been the focus of this chapter is ultimately the way people give meaning to the relevant occurrences, events and experiences in their lives. Agency is the emic meta-theory informing that process of signification. The world becomes understandable, events become humanised or at least imbued with value and meaning, through processes and problems that stem from ordinary daily social interaction. We live in a human world after all. If the world around us seems to be against us, to be thwarting our plans and rendering our lives insecure, it does so in a human way with meaning and a comprehensible intent. The attribution of agency to the "other" assures us that in this world we are almost at home.

References

Archer, Margaret (1996): *Culture and Agency. The Place of Culture in Social Theory*. Cambridge: Cambridge University Press.

Aronoff, Myron Joel (1976): *Freedom and Constraint. A Memorial Tribute to Max Gluckman*. Assen: van Gorcum.

Clough, Paul (2001): Conclusions: The Political Economy behind the Powers of Good and Evil. In: Clough, Paul and John P. Mitchell (eds): *Powers of Good and Evil. Social Transformation and Popular Belief*. New York: Berghahn, 233-252.

Cronk, Lee (1999): *That Complex Whole. Culture and the Evolution of Human Behavior*. Texas A & M: West View.

Ellis, Stephen and Gerrie ter Haar (2004): *Worlds of Power. Religious Thought and Political Practice in Africa*. London: Hurst.

Emirbayer, Mustafa and Ann Mische (1998): What is Agency? *American Journal of Sociology* 152 (2), 116-175.

Fortes, Meyer (1959): *Oedipus and Job in West African Religion*. In: Fortes, Meyer (ed.) (1983): *Oedipus and Job in West African Religion*. Cambridge: Cambridge University Press, 1-40.

Gell, Alfred (1998): *Art and Agency: An Anthropological Theory*. Oxford: Clarendon Press.

Giddens, Anthony (1990): *The Consequences of Modernity*. Cambridge: Polity Press.

Girard, René (1982): *Le bouc émissaire*. Paris: Grasset.

Horton, Robin (1959): Social Psychologies: African and Western. In: Fortes, Meyer (ed.) (1983): *Oedipus and Job in West African Religion*. Cambridge: Cambridge University Press, 41-89.

Meyer, Birgit (2001): 'You Devil, Go Away From Me!'– Pentecostal African Christianity and the Powers of Good and Evil. In: Clough, Paul and John P. Mitchell (eds): *Powers of Good and Evil. Social Transformation and Popular Belief*. New York: Berghahn, 104-134.

Mitchell, John P. (2001): *Introduction*. In: Clough, Paul and John P. Mitchell (eds.): *Powers of Good and Evil. Social Transformation and Popular Belief*. New York: Berghahn, 1-16.

Parkin, David (1985): *Introduction*. In: Parkin, David (ed.): *The Anthropology of Evil*. Oxford: Oxford University Press.

Reynolds-Whyte, Susan (1997): *Questioning Misfortune. The Pragmatics of Uncertainty in Eastern Uganda*. Cambridge: Cambridge University Press.

Thoden van Velzen, Bonno and Wilhelmina van Wetering (2001): *Dangerous Creatures and the Enchantment of Modern Life*. In: Clough, Paul and John P. Mitchell (eds): *Powers of Good and Evil. Social Transformation and Popular Belief*. New York: Berghahn, 17-42.

van Beek, Walter E. A. (2012a): Crab Divination among the Kapsiki/-Higi of North Cameroon and Northeastern Nigeria. In: Peek, Philip and Walter E. A. van Beek (eds.): *Reviewing Reality; Dynamics of African Divination*. Leiden: Brill, in press.

— (2012b): *The Dancing Dead; Ritual and Religion among the Kapsiki/Higi of North Cameroon and Northeastern Nigeria*. New York: Oxford University Press, in press.

— (2011): Medicinal Knowledge and Healing Practices among the Kapsiki/Higi of Northern Cameroon and Northeastern Nigeria In: Marleen Dekker & Rijk van Dijk, (eds.): Markets of well-being. Navigating Health and Healing in Africa. *African Dynamics* 9, 173-200.

— (2010): Eyes on top? Culture and the Weight of the Senses. In: Anne Storch (ed.): Invisible Africa. *Sprache und Geschichte in Afrika* 21, 245-270.

— (2009): The Healer and his Phone. Medicinal Dynamics among the Kapsiki of North Cameroon. In: Mirjam de Bruijn, Francis Nyamnyoh and Inge Brinkman (eds.): *Mobile Phones: The New Talking Drums of Everyday Africa*. Leiden: Langaa & African Studies Centre, 125-134.

— (2007): Agency in Kapsiki Religion. A Comparative Approach. In: de Bruijn, Mirjam, Rijk van Dijk and Jan-Bart Gewald (eds.): *Strength beyond Structure. Social and Historical Trajectories of Agency in Africa*. Leiden: Brill, 114-143.

— (2002): Why a Twin is not a Child; Symbolic Representations of Twinhood in Kapsiki. In: van Beek, Walter E. A., Jeanne-Françoise Vincent, Catharine Baroin and Paulette Roulon-Doko (eds.): L'enfant dans le bassin du Lac Chad. *Journal de la Société des Africanistes* 72 (1), 119-148.

— (1997): Rain as a Discourse of Power: Rainmaking in Kapsiki. In: Jungraithmayer, Herrmann, Daniel Barreteau and Uwe Seibert (eds.): *L'homme et l'eau dans le bassin du Lac Chad*. Paris: ORSTOM, 285-297.

— (1994): The Innocent Sorcerer; Coping with Evil in two African Societies, Kapsiki and Dogon. In: Blakely, Thomas D., Walter E. A. van Beek and Dennis L. Thomson (eds.): *African Religion: Experience and Expression*. London: James Currey, 196-228.

— (1992): The Dirty Smith; Smell as a Social Frontier among the Kapsiki/Higi of North Cameroon and North-Eastern Nigeria. *Africa* 2 (1), 38-58.

— (1987): *The Kapsiki and Higi of the Mandara Mountains*. Prospect Heights: Waveland Press.

Agency between Two Global Frames of Reference: Mozambican Students in Cuba and their Reintegration at Home

Hauke Dorsch

Strolling through Maputo's streets at an early stage of my research on Mozambicans who studied in Cuba[1], I was addressed by a young man, asking me whether I spoke English. He explained me that he worked in import and export, travelling between South Africa and Mozambique, and asked me if I were South African. When I answered that I came from Germany, the conversation switched immediately to German and he explained that he lived in Germany for a while and had family there. Then he asked whether I was a tourist in Mozambique, and I told him about the research. Again he changed languages, this time explaining in Spanish with an obvious Cuban accent that he studied for some years in Cuba. This was not just the situation every field researcher dreams of – not having to run after your informants but being approached by them – but additionally his story turned out to be extraordinary rich of agency, which is why I chose his biography as the starting point for this contribution that discusses the tension of Mozambican students' agency restricted by the strict application of a school discipline guided by the clash of two global frames of reference.

---

[1] This contribution is based on research conducted in the context of the SFB and its junior research group on South-South relations, directed by Katrin Hansing. We focussed on Cuban-African collaboration-ties in the fields of education and medicine. Katrin Hansing worked with Cuban doctors who "were on mission" (which is the official terminology) in different African countries or who still work in Mozambique and South Africa, whereas I spoke with students from a wide variety of African countries who today study in Cuba and with returnees in South Africa and Mozambique who went to school or universities in Cuba at some time during the last four decades. We conducted our research in Cuba, Mozambique and South Africa together, which is why I will often write of "us" when referring to field work situations. Furthermore I would like to stress that the following arguments benefited highly from our discussions on these subjects. I would like to thank our interviewees in Cuba, Mozambique and South Africa, without whom this work would not have been possible. With regards to Mozambique special thanks go out to Elísio Macamo. Earlier versions of this contribution focussed on the ritual aspects of these educational programmes (Dorsch 2008a), on the educational experience of crossing the Atlantic (Dorsch 2008b), and on the Mozambican students' experiences in Cuba and in Mozambique (Dorsch 2011).

Miguel, whose real name is of course not Miguel, lost his father at an early age and led a less than happy life with only little support from his sister's family. Once he heard of the possibility to study in Cuba, he decided that he would take this chance to obtain a free education. In 1985 at the age of 16 he came to the Isla de la Juventud, the Isle of Youth, to complete his secondary education in one of the four Mozambican schools on this small island a few kilometres south of mainland Cuba. Soon he became annoyed by the rigid discipline of the school and after some conflicts with his professors decided to leave the school and try to make a living on the main island. He travelled to Havana, slept in the streets, made friends with some Cubans, pretended to originate from Cuba's Oriente province and acquired a fake ID card that would allow him to move freely in Havana. He survived as what might be called a hustler, that is, he illegally sold goods to tourists, went shopping for Cubans who at the time were not allowed to enter "dollar-shops", which were accessible for him due to his foreign student identity card. He lived a thrilling life in Havana and Varadero, made friends with other hustlers and petty criminals until the day the police caught him and identified him as a foreign student. He was expulsed from Cuba and sent back to Mozambique. After only half a year of an indecisive life in Maputo he took the chance to get onto a flight to socialist Eastern Germany (the German Democratic Republic, GDR) by pretending that he finished his education in Cuba and was thus prepared to do the work in the GDR. As it turned out, the work was quite menial so he had no problems in performing it without a formal education. To his pleasure, he discovered that there were Cubans working in the same factory. Together they partied and dreamed in nostalgia of Cuba. After the fall of the Berlin wall he moved from East to West Berlin, then to Bavaria, married and had a child. Unfortunately the relationship broke up, which was why he left his family and went to work in South Africa and now travels constantly between South Africa and Mozambique. Back in Maputo he enjoys his friendship with Cubans and other Latin Americans and thus practises his Spanish. Enthusiastically, he listens to Cuban music and plays it as a DJ on Cuban parties.

Although his biography may not be what Mozambican and Cuban officials anticipated when they designed educational exchanges between the two countries, no doubt he leads a successful transnational life – and when asked about his wishes he says that he wants desperately to see his family in Germany but more than anywhere else he longs to go back to Cuba as soon as possible.

This introductory example will be grist for the mill of those who doubt that agency is a useful concept in social sciences, criticising the concepts' precedence of individuals over contexts, as an expression of the typical Western assumption of the triumph of will over contexts (e.g. Comaroff & Comaroff 1992: 10). Indeed Miguel's story sounds like an epic of the ideal Western individualist who in order to make his way creatively ignores or even uses the constraints created by cultural norms, laws or state institutions. It is thus all the more interesting that at the basis of Miguel's agency were frames of reference that shaped his Mozambican family values and his Cuban education, both supporting values other than your average Western individualism. In her discussion of the critique of the concept of agency, and focusing mainly on the Comaroffs, Sherry Ortner (2006) develops a concept of agency that allows for a fruitful analysis of individual or social action without ignoring the cultural context and the power structures that constrain or shape agency. Actually, she argues that agency as a concept necessarily contains the idea of a context – like culture for example – as a determinant of the goals of actions. But at the same time the context may be transformed by these actions. The goals that drive agency may be based on individual free will, but these goals and the accepted ways of achieving them are again shaped by cultural values, world views – or what we could call "frames of reference".[2] Apart from this idea of agency being culturally constructed, Ortner stresses the meaning of the concept of power with reference to agency and differentiates between agency as project or as resistance and agency as outcome of power. Another important aspect of her discussion is intentionality. Biological and other elementary needs or the Freudian unconscious might drive actions, but when speaking of agency, a conscious intention is usually implied. It is only in a footnote that Ortner (2006: 165, n6) refers to the idea of improvisation as a concept important for practice theory – which is unfortunate, because I think this to be an important aspect of agency. She discusses Pierre Bourdieu's concept of habitus as a set of limits within which an actor can improvise. In this interpretation, Ortner argues, improvisation is understood as being strongly guid-

---

2 See Roman Loimeier et al. 2005a for a definition of "frames of reference" and a discussion of the SFB's choice to use this concept and Loimeier et al. 2005b for an English version of this text.

ed by intentions, by consciously envisioned aims. Improvisation would just mean avoiding conventionally accepted ways, because they are not available to the actor and thus he or she creatively uses those opportunities at hand – an activity that Claude Lévi-Strauss (1962) described as bricolage. But another less intentional way of improvisation, Ortner reminds us, is comparable to the improvisation of a jazz musician – it is the improvisation for its own sake, for the aesthetic pleasure of playing with the possibilities available.

Keeping these reflections in mind, let us now turn towards the questions of this contribution: The main focus will be on the dominant world views or frames of reference and also the political contexts that shaped the programmes of sending African students to Cuba. I will show that agency was strictly constrained by institutional contexts. Therefore, I will describe those contexts, i.e. how the students were selected, sent abroad, assigned their subjects, sent back home and finally integrated into the work force – or in the latter case – how the state failed to do so. It is mainly at this point of return that Mozambican students' agency comes into play. We will have to ask what agency the students had, how the frames of reference in Cuba and Mozambique influenced the students' perception of their education and their chances to make a living in Mozambique. Finally, what was the influence of the change of these frames from the 1990s onwards? Unlike most contributions to this volume that focus on the encounter of a global and a local frame of reference, here we are confronted not with a local-global dichotomy or dialectic but with an interplay of at least two competing frames of reference with a global scope, i.e. socialist internationalism vs. neo-liberal globalisation. I write "at least", because apart from these two frames others come into play too: Christianity, Islam and colonialist modernity as we will see.[3]

[3] As this study focuses on the special situation of Mozambican students in Cuba and their return to Mozambique, the general questions on the influence of globalisation on education, although important in this context, cannot be discussed here. Suffice it to say that there is a growing number of studies on the migration of academics (Stichweh 2000a), on the global character of academia, the ideas of global standards of education and a growing commercialisation of universities (Stichweh 2000b, 2000c, Meyer and Ramirez 2000, Hayes and Wynyard 2002, Meyer 2005). With regard to the influence of globalisation on Cuban universities see Vazquez Castro and Dominguez 2002.

Two frames of reference – Cuba's activities in Africa as socialist internationalism or as an outcome of ancient blood bonds

In order to understand the interplay of these frames of reference we need at least a rough overview of the relations between the Cuban government and its African counterparts, which started in earnest only after the triumph of the Cuban revolution in 1959. The new government under the leadership of Fidel Castro quickly established close contacts with African independence movements and governments. Isolated from its "natural" sphere of interest, the neighbouring countries in the Caribbean, Central and South America, due to US hegemony in the American hemisphere, and because of the region's governments' fear of an export of the Cuban revolution, which these countries' governments later on saw exemplified in the Bolivian activities of Che Guevara and his fellow guerrilleros, Cuba turned to other countries of the South, mostly African and Asian countries that already showed some sympathies for socialist politics (Suchlicke & Fernandez 1985; D'Estfano et al. 1994; Ritter & Kirk 1995, Erisman 2000).

From 1961 onwards it supplied Algeria's National Liberation Front with arms and medical personnel and shipped wounded fighters and war-orphans to Cuba. In the same year Sékou Touré's Guinea was the first African country to send students to Cuba. In 1965 Cuba sent a group of Cuban guerrilleros led by Che Guevara to Congo-Kinshasa. But it was the long-lasting engagement in the Angolan fight for independence and the following civil war, and Cuba's military support against South African aggression in Namibia and Angola which probably most strongly shaped Cuba's image of itself as an internationalist nation leading the South. Interestingly Fidel Castro and other Cuban politicians and intellectuals justified this engagement in Africa not mainly with Cuban foreign political interests, and not only with expectable references to socialist internationalism, but also with the common historical experience of slavery and colonialism that African and Latin American countries shared, and also with the debt Cuba owes Africa because of African slaves' contributions to Cuban culture and in building the country. Castro extended this argument by referring to the "common blood" of Cubans and Africans (c.f. Castro 1989, Mandela & Castro 1991). Although greatly appreciated by authors from the African Diaspora, especially in the USA (cf. Walters 1993: 315), I guess it is fair to understand this "genealogical" or "biological frame of reference" as "mere" rhetoric, because for the students and Cubans active in the programmes the idea of this blood bond was not at all referred to, rather the idea prevailed, that Cuba as an advanced socialist nation supported the, as some interviewees said, "less developed" African nations.

Literacy and education programmes were seen as means to free the nations of the South from neo-colonial dependence from the North, mainly the US and Europe.[4] Thus, these Cuban contacts to other countries of the South must be interpreted in the wider context of Cold War politics as part of the socialist block's outreach for allies in Third World countries. Representing its revolution as an act of liberation from US neo-colonialism the Cuban government strongly emphasised its common interests especially with "radical" states such as Algeria, Congo-Brazzaville, Mali, Guinea and Ghana, as well as later on with the independence movements in the Portuguese colonies, which after they won their war of independence turned toward the socialist camp. The programmes of sending African students to Cuba were seen as part of the struggle between these two frames of reference – socialist internationalism as the world view and practice of the exploited peoples of the South and their allies in the socialist countries of Europe on the one hand, and on the other hand what was called imperialism and is today referred to as neo-liberal globalisation as world view and practice of the exploiting North (Gleijeses 2002: 30ff., 78, see also: Mesa-Lago & Belkin 1982, Gálvez 1999, Guevara 2000, Risquet Valdés 1999, 2000).

During the last 40 years the Cuban government signed agreements with governments or independence movements of nearly all Sub-Saharan African nations on the sending of students to Cuba. During the 1980s and 90s large numbers of primary, secondary and pre-university students were sent mostly to the Isla de la Juventud. They were assigned to schools erected especially for these foreign students. Usually each national group received one or more school buildings. The costs for these programmes were split, with Cuba paying the larger part, comprising education, accommodation, school uniforms, etc., and the sending countries' governments paying for travel expenses, their national teachers, and sometimes pocket money for the students (McManus 2000, Stubbs 1989: 98ff.). Following the collapse of the socialist camp in East Europe and Cuba's resulting economic problems, an era called the "special period" in Cuba, the number of foreign students dropped dramatically. There are only few sec-

4 On the Cuban literacy campaigns see Alexandra Keeble 2001.

ondary students from foreign countries remaining in Cuba now. However, many university students continue studying different careers, mostly Medicine or Nursing, but also Agriculture, Veterinary Medicine, Sports, Informatics, Social Communication, Law, Art, Film, Sociology, Spanish Language, Economy, Accountancy and others. Until the year 2000, 35.000 students from thirty-seven "Third World" countries have been schooled on "La Isla" (Risquet 2000: 96).[5]

According to numbers given to us by the Cuban Ministerio de Educación Superior nearly 43,000 foreign students finished their studies in Cuba on a secondary or university level between 1961 and 2004, of which nearly 30,000 came from sub-Saharan Africa. Of those, 8,053 came from Angola, the largest single national group, and still 3,764 from Mozambique. This changed recently. During our research, in the 2004-2005 semester, of the nearly 1,800 sub-Saharan African students that graduated in Cuba, there were for example 344 from South Africa, and more than 200 from Mali, but only less than 50 from Mozambique. Generally, the number of students sent by each nation was indicative of the political relations Cuba had with the respective African countries.

Mozambican students in Cuba – learning to follow the revolutionary vanguard

The recruitment of the students in Mozambique shows that the process of sending Mozambican students to Cuba was ideologically charged from the start. According to the statements of some former students, professors and officials in charge with the selection of students, academic merit and modest social background were the most important criteria for selection. Thus, at first children from rural, socially disadvantaged backgrounds who performed well at primary school were contacted and their parents were asked whether they would allow them to go to Cuba for secondary and eventually higher education. These seem to be very objective criteria, but when listening to the accounts of other, probably more critical former students, things sound a bit different: First of all there were already rumours – supposedly spread by South African media – that stu-

[5] Apart from the references cited, information on the establishment of the schools and the programmes for providing African students with education in Cuba were gathered during our field research in Cuba 09/2004 to 03/2005 and in Mozambique and South Africa from 08/2005 to 03/2006 through interviews with (former) students and professors and state officials in all three countries.

dents were subject to forced labour, even slavery in Cuba, that they were not to learn anything apart from being indoctrinated by socialist ideology. Additionally, some students told me there was some pressure on their parents to prove that they were not reactionaries who believed in these rumours, but that they were partisans of the FRELIMO, and thus would willingly give their children to support the development of the young nation.[6]

The FRELIMO, Liberation Front of Mozambique (Frente da Libertação da Moçambique), was at the time the governing party in a socialist one-party state. After gaining independence from Portugal in 1975 the FRELIMO government sought support mainly from the socialist camp, and from early on received aid from and sent students and workers to the Soviet Union, the GDR, Cuba and other mostly Eastern European socialist countries. After independence the FRELIMO government was militarily attacked by a group called RENAMO, the Mozambican National Resistance (Resistência Nacional Moçambicana) that was supported by South Africa's Apartheid government, which feared a socialist block at its borders (Dinerman 2006). Thus for Mozambican parents deciding whether they would send their children to Cuba or not implied the choice on whether they would side with FRELIMO or with RENAMO.

The idea behind this programme of sending students and teachers to Cuba was, given the lack of schools and school buildings in Mozambique, to have the students educated there as quickly as possible and then brought back as cadres. They would then be able to build up the country after the war of independence and in the face of continuing destabilisation from RENAMO forces. In order to

[6] The information on the process of selecting the students as well as on the daily lives in the Cuban schools was provided by former professors and a great number of former students in Mozambique who were sent to Cuba from 1977 onwards. The fear of students being indoctrinated by socialism rather than being educated "properly" is a wide-spread issue referred to by other authors, too (e.g. Nazario 1985: 88f.). Most of the (ex-) students interviewed had a slightly different perspective on this issue. Some in fact complained about a lack of political discussion in classrooms, rather than "over-politiciced" education, whilst others appreciated the additional historical and political information they received during their studies. Students spoke of the emphasis that was placed on issues such as: the common interests and struggles of third world countries, the importance of education, public health and social welfare for an independent nation. Many felt that what they learnt was patriotism rather than socialism and many said that they appreciated being made more aware of the needs of their homelands and local communities. For more information on education in Mozambique, see Mário 2003, Mazula 1995, Marshall 1993. For an overview of the higher education situation in Africa in general, see Zeleza & Olukoshi 2004.

give these children a sense of responsibility and urgency from the start, they were told that they were tomorrow's leaders of Mozambique and that they were to represent Mozambique in Cuba.[7]

In 1977 the first group was sent to Cuba, or more precisely to the Isla de la Juventud – where the first two school buildings had already been erected for them. Another two were about to follow. Each school had space for about 600 students. The age of the students differed mostly from 12 to 15 years of age (the oldest being in their twenties). All of them finished primary school in Mozambique and some had already started secondary school. In Cuba they received half a year of language training and then continued their school career. The last group was sent in 1990 – at the beginning of Cuba's so-called special period.

They were taught by Cuban as well as Mozambican teachers. The latter were brought there in order to keep students in contact with Mozambican culture. They taught Portuguese language, Mozambican history, geography with a focus on Africa and Mozambique and political education. The Cuban teachers taught Spanish, the Sciences, technical subjects, Sports, and Universal History. The aims of the education in secondary schools on the Isla were to teach a scientific, which meant of course: a materialist, world view and to educate revolutionary cadres. Following the dominant doctrine of national liberation, teachers tried to enforce national instead of regional, ethnic, local, or religious identities, which were seen as hindering a nation's development and were supposed to be used by reactionary forces in the interest of imperialism. This materialist and nationalist world view was not only taught in class but also "normalised" through extra-curricular activities. First the students were assigned to schools according to nationality. Contacts to students of other nationalities were reduced mostly to officially organised meetings. Students were encouraged to use Portuguese as the language of communication – to the effect that some forgot their maternal language. LPs – mostly with revolutionary songs praising the

7 Apart from the lack of school buildings and trained teachers in Mozambique there might have been other reasons why Cuban and Mozambican authorities did not decide to simply send Cuban teachers to Mozambique – as they did for example in Angola (Hatzky 2008). Although there were some attempts from the Cuban side to establish closer ties to Mozambique's FRELIMO, the relation remained somewhat distant, probably because of an unfortunate meeting of the FRELIMO's leader Eduardo Mondlane with Che Guevara in Dar-es-Salam in 1965. Whatever the reasons, Cuban teachers did not enter Mozambique or FRELIMO camps in Tanzania (Gleijeses 2002: 227ff).

FRELIMO – and newspapers were brought from Mozambique. These were meant to keep the students up to date on events in their home country, but also transmitted the national – and that meant: the governing party's – perspectives. Additionally the students were taught the dances of different provinces of Mozambique which they were to perform during regular events in other schools, be they Mozambican, Cuban, or of any other nation. The students thus had the different regions of their country inscribed into their bodies – they got to know the nation through sound and movement.

The ex-students characterised their Cuban teachers as being mostly very friendly, open and ready to develop personal relations, whereas the Mozambican teachers in comparison were described as being very authoritarian, strict, and distant. Apart from different pedagogic concepts at the basis of these differences in behaviour, one could argue that these were based in an evolutionist world view that put Cuba ahead in revolutionary development, whereas Mozambique was to prove its development: Mozambican teachers were in charge of the control of students, and this included that they felt responsible for proving to Cubans that Mozambican students too were disciplined revolutionaries. With regards to Mozambican society they were aware that a "reactionary" image prevailed that students from socialist countries did not have a profound education, that socialist education was not competitive enough, that all in all it was of lesser value than a Western education. The teachers thus felt the need to prove the excellence of their students with regard to both frames of reference.

These differences between Cuban and Mozambican teachers notwithstanding, school discipline in general was seen as being very strict. Discipline was a subject most interviewees referred to, it was presented to them as being at the basis of a revolutionary, modern society. They described everyday life in schools as being organised to the minutest detail in military-like manner: from the wake-up call at 6 o'clock in the morning to lights out at 10 pm. Apart from classes and homework it also included agricultural work. Even on weekends collective excursions were organised, but these were not compulsory for students.

Agricultural work as means to enforce national unity by overcoming the rural-urban divide was at the time still compulsory for Cuban students. This is of course the background of the rumours in Mozambique that students were being sold into slavery in Cuba, working in the fields instead of being educated.

Interestingly, most students had positive memories of this agricultural work; it seems that it was not very demanding. And it did not, as some rumours had it, pay the costs of the students' education.

An important aspect of this discourse on discipline was its negative definition: what was seen as lack of discipline. It included: not greeting teachers politely, leaving the school grounds, consuming alcohol or drugs, doing businesses with Cubans, committing crimes or acting in a violent manner, but also having sexual relationships, especially when resulting in pregnancy, wearing shirts bearing Western brandnames, or having too close a contact to those who were regarded as "indisciplinados", that is, persons lacking discipline. In severe cases, lack of discipline could result in public beatings or in being sent back to Mozambique without the possibility of finishing one's education in Cuba. Those sent back were received in Mozambique as counterrevolutionaries, and were sent to the provinces to do less attractive jobs. However, these strict concepts of discipline were applied less strictly over the years.

Those students who were successful enough in school to be asked to continue their studies in Cuba were sent to universities or polytechnics. Careers were not chosen by students, instead the Mozambican government applied for a certain number of positions in special careers. Cuba offered what it was able to grant, and students could choose between three or so careers and thus continue their studies on the main island. The life at universities and polytechnics was described as being of a less strict regimen. Mozambicans established closer contacts to Cubans and to students of other nationalities. They now received stipends from the Mozambican state and pocket money from the Cuban government. They were allowed to go out where and with whom they wanted, developed friendships and sexual relationships. Many felt that they had finally arrived in Cuba.

Materialist world views notwithstanding, religion was an important frame of reference for some of the students I talked to, and it was important even for the biographies of some of those who organised the educational programmes. Most leaders of the FRELIMO were educated in Catholic schools, which did not prevent them – like so many others before and after them – from readily embracing Marxism's materialist world view. The same holds true for some students today. Religion was not an issue for the early groups that went in the

70s, or so I was told. Like most of their Cuban co-students they had a materialist conviction and did not even think of going to church or mosque.

There were different responses more recently. I talked to Mozambican and other African Muslims who prayed regularly, kept the Ramadan, and tried to abstain from pork and alcoholic drinks. The latter was easy in secondary schools, as alcohol was forbidden anyway. But it seems that most university and polytechnic students usually found themselves immersed in Cuban culture – which with regard to food includes eating a great deal of pork, and drinking rum, of course. Other Muslim students managed to abstain from these "haram" seductions of Cuban life and concentrated on prayer meetings within their dormitories and other activities that would reinforce their Muslim identity. Christians on the other hand organised gatherings outside of school grounds or went to Catholic church services. The growing interest in religion among Cubans notwithstanding, the idealised image of Cuba being a revolutionary, materialist and secularised country is upheld in schools – and as such it is reproduced by most students. So there were only rare examples of African students being interested in Afro-Cuban religion for example. Actually students expressed annoyance of being approached by Cubans for background knowledge on Yorubá-deities, which Mozambicans clearly don't have.[8]

This leads us to another important aspect of Cuba's role in its propagated world view: its constantly proclaimed self-image of being a leader of the South, of having brotherly relations to African countries, and of being a non-racist society. How did African students experience this self-image in everyday life? Although some (former) students told me that, as Cuba was a "multi-racial" country and thanks to its egalitarian world view, there was no racism or xenophobia in Cuba, there were others who had different experiences. Some students encountered xenophobic situations, where Cubans threatened them or voiced the opinion that they should leave the country.[9] Many students complained about

---

[8] Yorubá denotes an ethnic group in Nigeria and Benin. The Afro-Cuban religion called Santería is based mainly on Yorubá cosmology. See e.g. Brown 2003, Fuentes & Gomes 2004.

[9] Cuba legally abolished all racial discrimination after the revolution. But this obviously did not change everybody's attitudes. Cuban official discourse of racial equality and of Cuba as a nation built on mestizaje, i.e. a mixture of African, European and to a lesser degree Native American and Asian cultures does not reflect everyday racism. In fact, it took the Cuban government until the 1990s to admit that the revolutionary aims of racial equality have not yet been achieved (de la Fuente 2001, McGarrity 1992, Hansing 2006).

Cubans' ignorance about Africa, that they met Cubans for example who thought that Mozambique was a province of Angola, that Africans lived in trees, that lions roamed African city streets, etc. Students criticised furthermore that images of Africa as a place of poverty, war, and wilderness were reproduced in Cuban television. Especially South African students, but also some Mozambicans, complained about the Cuban habit to address a black person in the street simply as "negrito" or "negrita"[10]. But even more educated Cubans, or those that knew an African country first-hand, expressed quite paternalist statements on Africa in interviews with us. They presented Cuba as the vanguard of international developments and as having the responsibility and fortunately the altruist internationalist world view that helped African countries find their way.

For nearly all students I spoke to, the voyage to Cuba was their first longer trip, and especially for those travelling by plane it was the first air flight. And I should add that for some – mostly from the first generation of students – it was also the first experience with wearing shoes, or school uniforms. Some used flushing toilets for the first time, some even received their first own shirts and trousers from the Mozambican government before embarking on their trip to Cuba. But most importantly, students were confronted with a highly structured day, a military-style life in the school, a strict regimen of time, discipline that was forcefully inflicted on their body – in a very Foucaultian way to modernisation, if you will. Thus everyday life in Cuba to some students from a rural background – differently to those coming from Maputo or other cities – meant their first close encounter with a modern lifestyle, or what some former students called civilisation.

This strict discipline and surveillance notwithstanding, students found ways to gain some personal freedoms. For example they took advantage of the less strictly regulated night hours to run away from their respective schools and visit other schools and befriend Cubans or students from other countries. When life in school became hardly bearable in the early 1990s because of Cuba's economic problems after the fall of the socialist camp resulting in a lack of food and other materials in the schools, students protested in order to receive a stipend. When these protests grew violent and teachers were injured a number of

[10] This translates as "little black male/female person". The diminutive is typical way of addressing people and not necessarily regarded as a sign of lack of respect.

students were sent home. But in the end the students succeeded in receiving their stipend. Once they were granted stipends in dollars they used this advantage to engage in business with Cubans, who at the time were not allowed to own dollars, and consequently were unable to buy the desired Western goods in the so-called dollar-shops. These businesses were a way of raising the students' stipends – and for some even a way of cheating their Cuban "business partners". In rare cases, students like Miguel ran away from the Isla and made it to the main island where they survived for some time before being expelled by Cuban authorities. These examples show that Mozambican students as individuals and as group found ways to circumvent strict control and used their abilities learned at school for other ends than those taught.

This contribution's title already hints at an uneasy in-between-ness. Should we speak of a clash of world views when referring to Mozambican students coming to Cuba? I don't think so: Apart from being very young and not yet having developed a stable world view, students coming from Mozambique in the 1970s and 80s were already in contact with socialist perspectives on society and history. Their preparation to their travel to Cuba included some months of living in camps in conditions comparable of those in Cuba, and they received some information about Cuba. Some students were brought up with a political background in FRELIMO contexts, thus the political education in Cuba, the materialist world view taught there, was just a continuation, deepening or radicalisation of their existing world view. Other students who went with less political knowledge appreciated political education as part of their general education probably without awareness of the Cuban bias in these political perspectives. A common frame of reference linked the Mozambican to the Cuban experience. This was to change when students returned home.

A returned elite in search of a position

If we believe the statements given to us by a Mozambican official from the ministry of education, the re-integration of the students into Mozambican society turned out to be very unproblematic (Interview, 22.1.2006). On their return the students were assigned to different work places according to their education if possible. They were readily accepted by their colleagues, their Cuban education was appreciated and respected, they were regarded as good professionals, as having discipline, and they turned out to be successful in their respective professional fields. They were ready to work in the provinces, whereas those educated in the West expected to continue to live the urban, metropolitan lifestyle they had become accustomed to in the West. Furthermore, unlike those who studied in the West, nearly all of those who studied in Cuba came back to Mozambique, not only thanks to the tight control in Cuba, but also because of the education that stressed patriotic responsibility and humbleness.

Of course, things appear a bit more problematic from the perspective of the students. It is important to note that from 1989 onwards the FRELIMO changed its politics, gradually evolving from what we may call a communist towards a social-democratic party and opening up the country for Western investment (Mazula 2000, Abrahamson & Nilsson 1995). From the start the "cubanitos" – small Cubans, as some former students call themselves, and I will use this term here – experienced doubts concerning the quality of their education, some even spoke of an especially bad image of Cuban or more general socialist education in Mozambique. As was referred to before, Cuban education was seen as being of lesser quality than Western education, as not being competitive enough for the new Mozambique. Therefore the cubanitos were confronted with the opinion that they received their jobs only because of their assumed closeness to the FRELIMO. Thus, they were forced right away to show their abilities and struggle for acceptance. Thanks to the quality of the education and their internalised discipline they were quite successful with it, many said. But, obviously they were not received as they were told they would be: as the country's future elite.

Today most of the cubanitos I spoke to were professionally well established: many had medium or upper level jobs in the public sector, but also in private enterprises. Some even started a business, which was enforced by the fact that most did not study what they wanted, but were assigned to subjects according to the supposed needs of the FRELIMO-government. But when students came back, the government was often unable to provide them with enough jobs in their respective fields – often because the infrastructure was destroyed due to the Civil War. Furthermore, students were desperately needed in other professional fields – or simply forced to join the army. Consequently, once they were free to choose work for themselves, many started a profession outside of the field they were educated in. Many interviewees stressed the fact, that despite the resistance and problems they faced when coming back, today one would find cubanitos who work as national directors, heads of departments, sectional heads, ministers, professors, presidents of city councils, etc. But there were others who complained about the lack of job arrangements from the state, which, they said, resulted in people with diplomas living on the street, doing menial jobs, thus in a waste of money and potential. The former students maintained the very Cuban or socialist idea that the state should provide its citizens with work, should help organise the individual's life, and should plan the economy and the work force. In fact, the country that many cubanitos left adhered to these principles, but when they returned it had opted for a more "Westernised" concept of the dynamic power of the free market.

This change notwithstanding, the students' education itself and their achieved abilities in different subjects allowed for a reorientation on the job market and a broad knowledge in sciences, philosophy, history and the arts, helped them make their way in modern Mozambican society. Being asked for their personal view on the value of the Cuban education and experience, many would mention that first of all it meant growing up, then that they were thankful for receiving an education, learning discipline, achieving a new (self-) consciousness as Mozambicans, as Africans, and, as some of them would say, becoming civilised through the knowledge of "classical literature" for example – or of table manners. They often described themselves in concepts of nationality, civilisation, modernity as opposed to others – especially those who did not receive an education – who were described with attributes like "tribal, local, backward, would eat with hands", etc. The students surprisingly used exactly those concepts which in colonial times differentiated an "assimilado" from an "indígena" in Portuguese diction.

Thus, in another respect the Cuban education turned out to be successful too: most interviewees stressed that thanks to their time in Cuba they returned as Mozambicans and not as Changan, Makonde, Northerner or Maputoan and that they have friends in different provinces who may help personally or professionally. Some were organised in associations for people who formerly studied in Cuba or in those with a general internationalist perspective. These associations organise events in memory of Mozambican or Cuban revolutionaries. Apart from keeping the memory of these individuals alive, these events also serve as nostalgic meetings of cubanitos. These meetings allowed communicating with other persons on common experiences and feelings of political or cultural estrangement from Mozambique.

It may be interesting to shortly refer to religion: Many returnees I talked to continued to abstain from church services. Others started going to church or the mosque again only out of politeness towards their families and stressed that their materialist world view was not in need of a deity. But a number of returnees said they found stability in religious belief, now that the values they were taught in Cuba were not much respected in Mozambique any more. Some found this stability in Evangelical churches which they described as being more serious in belief and practice than the Catholic church they were brought up with.

Coming back to the political changes in Mozambique between the 1980s and 1990s, we should ask how cubanitos experienced the different frames of reference in 1970s or 80s Mozambique and Cuba on the one hand and in 1990s Mozambique on the other hand. According to their own accounts they brought back an idea of modernity that was characterised by patriotism, collectivism, altruism, discipline, and the like and tried to integrate these values into their private and professional lives, that is, strive to positions of responsibility according to these values. Confronted with the obvious differences in values of their socialist education and their capitalist everyday lives and thus with the different rules of "serious games" as Sherry Ortner (1996, 2006) would call it, many of the interviewees either talked about the need to adapt – or they simply denied these differences through reference to shared values like modernity: they stressed the role cubanitos played in developing the country, one interviewee even stated: "The Cuban education is at the basis of Mozambican modernisation." Another cubanito offered a rather wide definition of Socialism as being a social process guided by sciences and thus concluded that Mozambique was on its own way to constructing socialism[11]. These strategies to bridge cognitive dissonances between the respective world views may have functioned as ways of negotiating the two different educative experiences – or to put it biographically: the two identities of being at the same time Cuban and Mozambican. Thus it is no surprise that most interviewees spoke of two homelands they had, and nearly all expressed the wish to at least visit Cuba one day.

[11] Interview A.M., 16.10.2005; interview A.Q., 19.12.2005.

Conclusion

Coming back to the title's question let me try to analyse this special situation of an interaction not of a global and a local frame of reference or world view but of two frames with a global scope: socialist internationalism and neo-liberal globalisation, formerly known as imperialism (from its enemies' perspective). From the start the educational programmes were shaped by the binary or dichotomist world view which manifested itself on different levels as follows:

First, on the global level there was the idea of a universal struggle between the forces of imperialism and those of the exploited. Cuban or Soviet support for Mozambique – and also what in Cuba is dubbed South-South-Solidarity – were understood as decidedly anti-imperialist or anti-neo-colonial practices and continue to be propagated as an alternative to the exploitative aspects of globalisation.

Second, on the national level this dichotomist world view manifested itself as an on-going struggle between these progressive and reactionary forces – be it the Civil War in Mozambique and its antagonistic protagonists FRELIMO and RENAMO but also in Cuba which cultivates a continuous state of vigilance against a possible US-backed invasion from Cuban exiles in Miami. It is this context which may help us understand why military discipline was upheld in the schools the way I described it, why religious beliefs or ethnic identifications were regarded as reactionary – or why even wearing a T-shirt with a Western brandname was regarded as a counter-revolutionary act. It also helps us understand the mistrust cubanitos received from Mozambicans who were critical about FRELIMO's orientation toward the socialist block.

It is interesting to see that these two frames of reference that seemingly exclude each other were successfully negotiated on the third level, that of identity. Thanks to Cuban education, cubanitos said, they gained modernity, nationality, civilisation. And probably because of the common roots of both frames of reference in Enlightenment and Humanism this education helped them make their way in Mozambique. We may try to explain the disturbing closeness of Cuban socialist and Portuguese colonial values concerning the idea of what defines a civilised person. We may also analyse Cuban official political discourse as yet being unquestioned by post-modern interventions. We will find few examples of Black Atlantic countercultural positions (Gilroy 1993, Hansing 2006), but rather an on-going everyday racism in Cuba and paternalist positions among its elites, which may be explained through their roots in modernist and especially Marxist evolutionist ideology. These positions may seem conservative or disturbing for us academics more or less influenced by post-modern perspectives – but it seems that they at least helped many Mozambicans who returned from Cuba finding their position in a modernised African society changed by globalisation.

When recounting Miguel's activities for making a living in Cuba, Germany, South Africa and Mozambique as an introduction to this contribution, I did so in order to stress the point that, although the students were strongly influenced by the two competing global frames of reference and their agency was determined by the need to negotiate these, improvisation did play an important role. Despite his problematic experiences with Cuban authorities, Miguel continued to support Cubans in Mozambique and highly appreciated Cuban culture – and thus probably turned out to be closer to the ideal of the altruist humanist of the South than many Cubans and Africans active in these programmes, who over the years became quite cynical about its outcomes (see Dorsch & Hansing 2005). He also improvised with the possibilities at hand. His improvisations are of course an extreme example of how far an individual's action could overcome or use the constraints put in his way by the state, which is why I chose them as a contrast to my account of students' agency being restricted by the dominant frames of reference. In ending, let me come back to Sherry Ortner's point that improvisations may be both a means to an end and an end in themselves. When speaking to Miguel I gained the impression that his improvisations were without doubt intentionally directed to a goal: the bettering of his economic situation. But obviously he also delighted in overcoming obstacles through unconventional means and no doubt it provided him with aesthetic pleasure to tell stories about how he managed to do so.

References

Abrahamsson, Hans and Anders Nilsson (1995): *Mozambique – The Troubled Transition from Socialist Construction to Free Market Capitalism*. London et al.: Zed Books.

Brown, David (2003): *Santería Enthroned – Art, Ritual, and Innovation in an Afro-Cuban Religion*. Chicago: The University of Chicago Press.

Castro, Fidel (1989): *We Are United by Blood*. In: Deutschmann, David (ed.): *Changing the History of Africa - Angola and Namibia*. Melbourne: Ocean Press.

Comaroff, John L. and Jean Comaroff (1992): *Ethnography and the Historical Imagination*. Boulder: Westview Press.

de la Fuente, Alejandro (2001): *A Nation for All – Race, Inequality, and Politics in Twentieth-Century Cuba*. Chapell Hill & London: The University of North Carolina Press.

D'Estefano Pisani, A.Miguel, José M.Galego Montano and Carmen Solana Valdés del María (eds.) (1994): *Fidel y el Tercer Mundo*. Hanoi: Editorial Chnih Tri Quoc Gia.

Dinerman, Alice (2006): *Revolution, Counter-Revolution and Revisionism in Postcolonial Africa – The Case of Mozambique 1975-1994*. New York & London: Routledge.

Dorsch, Hauke (2008a): Übergangsritus in Übersee? Zum Aufenthalt mosambikanischer Schüler und Studenten in Kuba. *Afrika Spectrum* 43 (2), 225-242.

— (2008b): Studierende und Schüler aus dem südlichen Afrika in Kuba – Navigieren zwischen Rotem und Schwarzem Atlantik. *Ethnoscripts* 10 (1), 7-29.

— (2011): Red or Black Atlantic? Mozambican Students in Cuba and their reintegration at home. *Zeitschrift für Ethnologie* 136 (2).

Erisman, H. Michael (2000): *Cuba's Foreign Relations in a Post-Soviet world*. Gainesville: University of Florida Press.

Fuentes Guerra, Jesús and Grisel Gómez (2004): *Cultos Afrocubanos – Un estudio etnolingüístico*. Havana: Editorial de Ciencias Sociales.

Gilroy, Paul (1993): *The Black Atlantic Modernity and Double Consciousness*. Cambridge: Harvard University Press.

Gleijeses, Piero (2002): *Conflicting Missions: Havana, Washington, and Africa, 1959-1976*. Chapel Hill: University of North Carolina Press.

Che Guevara, Ernesto (2000): *The African Dream – The Diaries of the Revolutionary War in the Congo*. London: Harvill.

Hansing, Katrin (2006): *Rasta, Race and Revolution – The Emergence of the Rastafari Movement in Socialist Cuba*. Münster: LIT Verlag.

Hansing, Katrin and Hauke Dorsch (2005): 45 Jahre Süd-Süd-Solidarität? Cubanische Mediziner in Afrika, afrikanische Studenten in Cuba. *Ila* 291 (December 2005/ January 2006), 10-13.

Hatzky, Christine (2008): "Os bons colonizadores" Cuba's Educational Mission in Angola, 1976-1991. *Safundi – The Journal of South African and American Studies* 9 (1), 53-68.

Hayes, Dennis and Robin Wynyard (eds.) (2002): *The McDonaldization of Higher Education*. Westport & London: Bergin & Garvey.

Keeble, Alexandra (2001): *Con el espíritu de los maestros ambulantes – La campaña de la alphabetización Cubana, 1961 / In the Spirit of wandering Teachers –- Cuban Literacy Campaign, 1961*. Melbourne, New York & Havana: Ocean Press.

Lévi-Strauss, Claude (1962): *La pensée sauvage*. Paris: Plon.

Loimeier, Roman, Dieter Neubert and Cordula Weißköppel (eds.) (2005a): *Globalisierung im lokalen Kontext – Perspektiven und Konzepte von Handeln in Afrika*. Berlin, Hamburg & Münster: LIT Verlag.

— (2005b): *Globalization in the Local Context – Perspectives* and *Action in Africa – An Introduction*. Available online: <http://www.opus.ub.uni-bayreuth.de/volltexte/2005/171/pdf/loimeier_komplett_27_07.pdf.>

Mandela, Nelson and Fidel Castro (1991): *How Far We Slaves Have Come!* New York et al.: Pathfinder.

Mário, Mouzinho, Peter Fry, Lisbeth Levey and Arlindo Chilundo (2003): *Higher Education in Mozambique*. Oxford: James Currey; Maputo: Imprensa & Livraria Univeritária, Uni-versidade Eduardo Mondlane.

Marshall, Judith (1993): *Literacy, Power, and Democracy in Mozambique – The Governance of Learning from Colonization to the Present*. Boulder et al.: Westview Press.

Mazula, Brazão (1995): *Educação, cultura e ideologia em Moçambique: 1975-1985*. Porto: Fundo Bibliográfico da Língua Portuguesa/Edições Afrontamento.

— (2000): *A construção da democracia em Africa – O caso Moçambicano*. Maputo: Ndjira.

McManus, Jane (2000): *Cuba's Island of Dreams – Voices from the Isle of Pines and Youth*. Gainesville: University Press of Florida.

McGarrity, Gayle (1992): Race, Culture, and Social Change in Contemporary Cuba. In: Halebsky, Sandor, John M. Kirk, Carollee Bengelsdorf, Richard L. Harris and Andrew Zimbalist (eds.): *Cuba in Transition: Crisis and Transformation*. Boulder: Westview Press, 193-205.

Mesa-Lago, Carmelo and June S. Belkin (eds.) (1982): *Cuba in Africa*. Pittsburgh: University of Pittsburgh.

Meyer, John W. (2005): *Weltkultur – Wie die westlichen Prinzipien die Welt durchdringen*. Frankfurt/M: Suhrkamp.

Meyer, John W. and Francisco O. Ramirez (2000): The World Institutionalization of Education. In: Schriewer, Juergen (ed.): *Discourse Formation in Comparative Education*. Frankfurt/M: Peter Lang, 111-132.

Nazario, Olga (1985): Cuba's Relations with Africa in the Eighties: Scope and Limitations. In: Suchlicke, Jamie and Damian J. Fernandez (eds.): *Cuban Foreign Policy: The New Internationalism*. Coral Gables: University of Miami, North South Center for the Institute of Interamerican Studies, 68-98.

Ortner, Sherry (1996): Making Gender – Toward a Feminist, Minority, Postcolonial, Subaltern, etc., Theory of Practice. In: Ortner Sherry: *Making Gender – The Politics and Erotics of Culture*. Boston: Beacon Press, 1-20.

— (2006): Power and Projects – Reflections on Agency. In: Ortner, Sherry: *Anthropology and Social Theory – Culture, Power and the Acting Subject*. Durham & London: Duke University Press, 129-153.

Risquet Valdés, Jorge (1999): *40 años de solidaridad de Cuba con África*. Havana: Editorial Si-Mar.

— (2000): *El segundo frente del Che en el Congo - Historia del Batallón Patricio Lumumba*. Havana: Casa Editora Abril.

Stichweh, Rudolf (2000a): Von der "Peregrinatio Academica" zur globalen Migration von Studenten. Nationale Kultur und funktionale Differenzierung als Leitthemen. In: Stichweh, Rudolf: *Die Weltgesellschaft – Soziologische Analysen*. Frankfurt/M: Suhrkamp, 146-169.

— (2000b): Globalisierung der Wissenschaft und die Rolle der Universität. In: Stichweh, Rudolf: *Die Weltgesellschaft – Soziologische Analysen*. Frankfurt/M: Suhrkamp, 130-145.

— (2000c): Gibt es eine „Weltpolitik" der „Weltwissenschaft"? In: Stichweh, Rudolf: *Die Weltgesellschaft – Soziologische Analysen*. Frankfurt/M: Suhrkamp, 170-183.

Stubbs, Jean (1989): *Cuba – The Test of Time*. London: Latin American Bureau.

Suchlicke, Jamie and Damian J. Fernandez (eds.) (1985): *Cuban Foreign Policy: The New Internationalism*. Coral Gables: University of Miami, North South Center for the Institute of Interamerican Studies.

Vázquez Castro, Fernando and Jorge J. Domínguez Menéndez (2002): Globalización, internacionalización y cooperación Inter-institucional a nivel nacional, regional y internacional. In: Martín Sabina, Elvira (ed.): *La educación superior de Cuba en la década del 90*. La Habana: Editorial Félix Varela.

Walters, Ronald W. (1993): *Pan Africanism in the African Diaspora: An Analysis of Modern Afrocentric Political Movements*. Detroit: Wayne State University Press.

Zeleza, Paul Tiyambe and Adebayo O. Olukoshi, (eds.) (2004): *African Universities in the Twenty-first Century*. 2nd ed. Dakar: CODESRIA /UNISA Press.

Islamic Religious Endowments (*waqf*) in Colonial Zanzibar

Norbert Oberauer

Introduction

This chapter deals with an Islamic institution called *waqf*, which is commonly referred to in English as "religious endowment". More precisely, the chapter will focus on the local history of that institution in 19th and early 20th century Zanzibar. We shall see, however, that the history of waqf in Zanzibar was not "local" in any strict sense of the word. Rather, it resulted from a complex interaction of both local and transregional influences. Endowing waqf became a common social practice in Zanzibar in the first part of the 19th century, when the Omani Sultan Sayyid SaÝĐd established his rule over large parts of the Swahili Coast. Omani rule involved significant shifts in the political, social and economic structure of coastal societies. The introduction of waqf into the local context and the specific patterns of endowment practice prevailing in Zanzibar reflect this newly emerging socio-economic structure. Waqf was intimately linked to a new class of wealthy patron families who used religious endowments to foster bonds of dependence and loyalty with manifold clientele.

However, political and socio-economic conditions shifted anew when Zanzibar became a British protectorate in 1890. British officials disapproved of the informal ties between patrons and clients, who in British eyes should turn into entrepreneurs and wage labourers. As a consequence, the colonial power imposed an administration of waqf which proved disruptive to traditional patterns of endowment practice.

To present the history of waqf in Zanzibar, I shall proceed in three steps: First, I give a brief account of the institution of waqf as such and its place in Islamic social and legal history. Then, I describe the historical introduction of waqf into the local context of Zanzibar and depict the prevalent patterns of local endowment practice. Finally, I give an outline of British waqf policy and illustrate its effects on local waqf practice.

Waqf as an Islamic legal institution

Islamic religious endowment practices date back at least to the 2nd century of Islam. Over the subsequent centuries, Islamic scholars developed a specific legal framework for religious endowment.[1] Waqf law forms part of the written legal tradition of Islam, which over the centuries became a normative frame of reference for practically the entire Islamic world.

According to Islamic law, a Muslim may divest himself of some property, declaring it waqf. The property thereby becomes inalienable: it must not be mortgaged or sold and must, according to some jurists, be conceived of as "God's property".[2] However, a waqf can still be used or rented out, and thus may produce income. In principle, any object may be dedicated as a waqf, although most jurists require that the object is durable. This requirement excludes the endowment of goods whose use consists in their consumption, but it does not – according to most jurists – exclude the endowment of animals or slaves. In practice however, by far the most waqf endowments in history consisted of real estate.

When a waqf is donated, the founder usually stipulates a purpose of dedication. Income derived from the waqf must not be spent for any other purpose. The purpose of a waqf can be the upkeep of an institution – typically a mosque or an institution of religious learning. In fact, in Islamic history the production of religious knowledge was to a great extent financed through waqf, which provided a material basis for scholarship independent from political rule. Apart from institutions, a founder of a waqf may also stipulate persons as beneficiaries, as for instance freed slaves or – which is most common – the founder's own offspring. In that latter case the benefit of the waqf reverts from one generation of the founder's children to the next. All waqf, however, turns into waqf for the benefit of the poor when the stipulated beneficiaries become extinct. Thus, all waqf implies an ultimate gift to charity.

In many historical Muslim societies endowing waqf was a wide-spread social practice. Waqf in favour of religious institutions presented a means for rulers and other elites to legitimise their leading position in society and at the same

---

1 For the emergence of waqf as a legal institution see Hennigan 2004 and Peters 2002.

2 For an outline of the classical Islamic doctrine regarding waqf see Peters 2002, with further references.

time to exert some influence on religious discourse. Waqf in favour of dependents, in turn, was very popular mainly for two reasons: For one thing, such waqf presented a means to bypass the rigid rules of the Islamic law of inheritance. In Islamic law, a testator can dispose of only one third of his property by will. The rest is divided among the relatives according to fixed shares, which entails that property is increasingly split up over generations. By founding a waqf one could pass the benefit of one's property to whomever one liked, and at the same time avoid the property's fragmentation. Furthermore, Islamic law proscribes to touch a waqf or its proceeds in order to settle any debts run up by the beneficiaries. Accordingly, to provide one's offspring with waqf meant to provide them with secure income. Endowed property was saved from the risks of commercial ups and downs, just as it was saved from the offspring's prodigality.

As for the administration of waqf, it usually rests with a trustee, called mutawallĐ in Arabic. A mutawallĐ must be a trustworthy Muslim and, according to most schools of law, male. Ordinarily, the trustee is appointed by the founder, who may also lay down rules for the appointment of future trustees. The trustees, however, must be supervised by the QÁÃĐ, who has the duty to safeguard the proper administration of endowments and to step in as a trustee himself if a waqf is not properly managed.

Waqf in the local context of traditional Zanzibar

In historical Zanzibar, by far the most common kinds of waqf were endowments for the upkeep of mosques and endowments for the benefit of the founder's offspring.

We cannot tell with certainty how far the practice of endowing waqf dates back on the Swahili coast. There is no evidence of endowment activity prior to the 19th century, but this lack of evidence might simply result from the general scarcity of historical data available for the region. What is certain is that endowing waqf became a very widespread social practice during the first decades of the Omani Sultanate of Zanzibar – that is after the Omani Sultan SaÝĐd established his rule over large parts of the Swahili Coast in the 1820s. Towards the end of the century, when the British colonial power gradually seized control of the Sultanate, a substantial amount of Zanzibar's real estate had been turned into waqf. There are no precise figures on waqf from the early phase of the Protectorate, but a survey undertaken in 1944 records that more than 6% of the houses in Zanzibar Stone Town (the Sultanate's capital) were waqf.[3] To this must be added a considerable amount of urban space dedicated for the free dwelling of the poor or as burial grounds for the local elites.[4]

The boom of waqf under Omani rule is not a coincidence. Under Omani rule, the political and economic conditions of the Swahili Coast greatly shifted. That shift resulted in a social structure in which the institution of waqf could fulfil a number of important functions.

Omani rule brought three main changes to coastal society: Firstly, the introduction of large scale cash crop production – mainly cloves; secondly, a significantly enhanced involvement of coastal economy with the global capitalist market; and thirdly, the emergence of new economic and political elites, mainly of Arab origin, but to some extent also of Indian and Swahili origin. These new elites were those who controlled the most important sources of economic wealth: plantations, capital to invest in long distance trade, and access to the extensive commercial networks that spread out to the various littorals of the Indian Ocean.[5]

Political power in the Sultanate was essentially rooted in economic power. Political authority was fostered by what Randall Pouwels has styled "largesse", viz. a barely formalised redistribution of wealth in exchange for political loyalties and support.[6] The political structure that emerged from "largesse" may best be described as a system of patronage. Even the Sultan as the nominal sovereign was little more than the "biggest patron" of the region.[7] He was a *primus inter pares*, whose power over other wealthy families was comparatively limited. His power did not rest on any large standing army. Nor did it rest on descent, as the IbÁÃÐ creed of Oman precluded descent as a legitimising factor for rule. It rested mainly on the enormous personal wealth of the Sultan, as well as on his

3 See Sheriff 2001: 33.

4 On burial grounds in Zanzibar see Issa 1995: 70. On waqf land dedicated for the free dwelling of poor see ZNA, HD 3/5, HD 5/9 and HD 10/13, as well as the decision in Civil Case No. 1333 of 1907, The Wakf Commissioners for Zanzibar v. Wallo Ramchor, reported in Z.L.R. 1, 227-239.

5 For an account of the establishment of Omani domination on the Swahili coast see Pouwels 1987.

6 See Pouwels 1987: 102 and 108.

7 For the political role of the Sultan see Pouwels 1987: 103 ff.

entrepreneurial skills. It was these sources of power that made British observers speak of the Sultan as a "merchant prince".

The Sultan represented just one of many wealthy families who used "largesse" to foster their political and economic position. Wealthy families dominated specific urban and rural spaces, building and maintaining a local mosque, and fostering bonds of loyalty and dependence with all kinds of people less economically blessed then themselves. Thus, wealthy families formed the centre of socio-economic units which went far beyond mere kinship-ties.[8] At the same time, such families enjoyed a considerable degree of autonomy vis-à-vis the Sultan.

The manifold clientele of such patron families consisted to a large extent of slaves. The cash crop plantations created a strong demand for labour which was met by importing large numbers of slaves from the East African mainland. At the middle of the 19th Century, slaves formed roughly two thirds of Zanzibar's population.[9] To speak of slaves as "clients" is of course euphemistic. However, even slaves enjoyed some marginal rights within the normative framework of local custom. Thus in 1906, a high ranking British official observed that "an Arab who discarded an old or sick slave would [...] be regarded with contempt by his associates, and such an occurrence is very exceptional".[10] Besides, slaves were frequently manumitted by their owners.[11] Usually the freed slaves chose to continue in their former owner's services – partly because there was no viable economic alternative. All in all, the sources suggest that aside from the voluntariness of a patron-client-relationship, clientship and slavery carried rather similar features: Both clients and slaves enjoyed certain rights, but both strongly depended on the master or patron in economic terms.

To sum up: The social structure of the Sultanate was essentially shaped by notions of patronage, and this applies to all strata of society, including the ruling elite. Now as for waqf, that institution presented a perfect medium for wealthy families to act out their role as patrons. Not only was it an excellent means to

---

8 See Pouwels 1987: 78.

9 See Cooper 1977: 56.

10 See Memorandum to the Foreign Office by the British Agent and Consul General Basil Cave, FO 881/9215, p. 41. Cooper, too, in his study on slavery in Zanzibar, describes the notions of mutual loyalty and responsibility between masters and slaves as a characteristic feature of slavery in the Sultanate (see Cooper 1977: 162, 183, 246).

11 See Fair 2001: 115 f., Cooper 1977: 243 and 252.

display largesse, it also provided largesse with an explicit reference to Islam as the predominant normative discourse. In short: waqf was excellently suited for the social and economic power structures emerging in Zanzibar under Omani domination, and this accounts for the rapid growth of endowment activity in the first decades of the Sultanate.

However, the new patron class of Zanzibar did not simply adopt the legal concept of waqf. They also adapted it to local conditions, and this adaptation involved some deviations from classical legal doctrine.

For one thing, there was virtually no official supervision of waqf administration in the Sultanate. The Sultan and his QÁÃĐs very rarely interfered into waqf matters. It will be remembered that according to Islamic law, the QÁÃĐ has a duty to safeguard the proper administration of waqf, and thus the lack of official supervision of waqf in Zanzibar was not strictly in line with legal doctrine. On the other hand, the far reaching autonomy of patron families in the Sultanate presumably precluded any regular official interference in waqf matters. As a rule, waqf was administered by its founder's heirs, who considered waqf a "family issue" that was no business of the ruler or his representatives.

There were other deviations from classical waqf doctrine which were more substantial: In applying waqf resources, families usually did not adhere very strictly to the founder's express stipulations. Waqf formally dedicated for the founder's offspring was frequently used to accommodate the various clients and dependents of the family, including slaves and ex-slaves. Those dependants were allowed to live on waqf land rent free or in waqf houses for a merely nominal rent.[12] This practice did of course not present a breach of Islamic law, but merely a very generous use of resources which nominally were reserved for the founder's offspring. However, virtually all kinds of waqf were used in that fashion – including waqf formally dedicated for entirely different purposes, like for instance mosque upkeep.[13] Such waqf, too, was controlled by the founder's family who customarily used it to accommodate their manifold clientele. In short: All kinds of waqf were effectively treated as a family resource, though

[12] See for instance ZNA, HD 6/55, as well as Z.L.R. 1, p. 227-239, The Wakf Commissioners for Zanzibar v. Wallo Ramchor, and Z.L.R. 1, 366, Ali bin Nassor bin Khalad v. Zwena binti Hamood.

[13] See ZNA, AB 34/1, particularly Clarke to Shearman Turner on 18th of February 1913.

one earmarked for the kind of largesse that fostered the family's social standing as patrons.

This practice was a clear deviation from written Islamic legal tradition, which prescribes strict adherence to the founder's stipulations. However, the indifferent use of waqf as a "charitable family resource" did not reflect a plain disregard of Islamic law. Rather, that practice must be understood as a local contextualisation of Islamic law. It is important to see that the people of Zanzibar usually did not perceive that practice as "unislamic". In their eyes, religion required of a patron family to provide for both a local mosque and for their needy clientele. Both issues were part and parcel of a patron's manifold social obligations. As long as those obligations were met, it was of little practical importance which of the family's resources was used for which specific purpose.

To sum up: while patron families in the Sultanate drew on Islamic waqf law as a normative frame of reference, they also adapted that law to local conditions and, in particular, to the patterns of patronage prevailing in local society.

British interference in local waqf practice

In 1890 the Sultanate was turned into a British Protectorate. British officials had little sympathy for the local patterns of endowment practice. Judging from colonial administrative files, it is doubtful whether those officials actually understood the traditional concept of waqf. At any rate, they disapproved of local waqf practice and felt the need to interfere.

Significantly, the British from the very beginning referred to waqf as "charities". Yet by-and-by they had to realise that the purpose of a waqf was not always "charity" as they conceived it. British officials conceived of "charity" in terms of public welfare, as opposed to "family care", which in British eyes was a private issue. According to this conceptual distinction, a waqf dedicated for the founder's offspring did not qualify as "charity". Such a waqf was rather – to use the words of a high ranking British judge – a "veiled means of mere family aggrandizement",[14] or – as the British Resident disdainfully put it – a "fantastic

---

[14] The expression was used by a judge of the Privy Council in the Council's decision on Mahomed Ahsanulla Chowdry v. Amarchand Kundu, (1890) 17 Cal., 498. The decision is quoted in the judgment of the court in Suleman bin Ahmed v. Salim bin Abdalla el-Wardi, H.B.M. Court for Zanzibar, Civil Case No. 1546 of 1908, Z.L.R. 1, 328-333.

charity".[15] Yet what was even more irritating to British officials was the fact that the "real charities" – such as waqf for the upkeep of mosques – were treated as family resources, too. In British eyes, that practice amounted to simply an abuse of charitable resources. It meant – as one British official put it – "robbing Him [God] of what is due for the upkeep of the buildings dedicated for Him and for the support of those who are emphatically styled 'God's poor'".[16]

This British point of view disregarded, however, that neither the British concept of charity, nor the British concept of a family made much sense against the background of Zanzibar social structure. A Zanzibari stricken by poverty did not turn to any such thing as "charity" – he became the client of a wealthy patron. That patron, in turn, carried social obligations clearly going beyond those of a "family head". He stood at the centre of a large social unit confined not by blood relationship, but by dependence and loyalty.

At this point it becomes rather clear that waqf and the question of how to properly administer it had a lot to do with concepts of social order. It had to do with social roles defined by specific rights and responsibilities. The terms "patron" and "client" point to such roles. Equally, such roles are implicit to modern concepts of family and charity. The "modern family" is a small kinship unit which is supposed to be economically self-reliant. It is thus autonomous vis-à-vis other families. To safeguard that autonomy, charity must be provided as public welfare, and not by the hands of other families. In short: welfare provided by personal largesse of patrons defied British notions of how a society should function. And this is one reason why British officials deemed the local waqf practice of Zanzibar unacceptable.

The colonial administration did not plainly abolish waqf as a legal institution. Such a drastic step would have been unadvisable in terms of political strategy, which called for caution not to affront local religious sensitivities too harshly. Instead, British officials came up with their own interpretation of Islamic waqf law – an interpretation much more in line with British concepts of charity and family care. The British pointed out that the written Islamic legal tradition commands strict compliance with the stipulations of the founder. On that legal basis the British felt justified to introduce a strict separation between

---

15 ZNA, AB 34/1, Clarke to Shearman Turner on 18th of February 1913.

16 ZNA, AB 34/1, anonymous Memorandum, undated (but before 1914). I have added the word "God" in parantheses for the sake of clarity.

what they came to call "Family-Waqf", on the one hand, and "Charitable Waqf" on the other. At the same time, the British administration compelled trustees to manage all waqf on "strict business lines". Waqf was to be exploited to the fullest by charging maximum rents from the various tenants. Houses were no longer to be rented out on nominal rents, and owners of huts situated on waqf-land were now charged a ground rent. In other words: Largesse had to yield to economic efficiency.[17] Trustees who refused to adopt that business attitude were threatened to be deprived of their position as trustees on the grounds of "mismanagement". They ran a risk to have their waqf taken over by a so-called "Waqf Commission", an administrative body instituted by British legislation and controlled by British officials. The income derived from such "business-like" management was to be divided in strict accordance with the founder's stipulations: In case of a "Family-Waqf" the proceeds had to go exclusively to the founder's offspring, whereas in case of a "Charitable Waqf" all income had to serve the stipulated charitable purpose – usually mosque upkeep. In short: The British enforced their concepts of "family-care" and "charity" as mutually exclusive categories by seizing control of the flow of waqf resources, and redirecting that flow accordingly.

Up to this point I have depicted the history of waqf in colonial Zanzibar as a mere clash of concepts – a clash of culturally forged norms regarding social roles and responsibilities. It is important to see, however, that those concepts were not devoid of material interests. After all, waqf presented a considerable economic resource.

To exploit charitable waqf on business lines provided ample resources for the upkeep of mosques. To mobilise such resources was in fact an important interest of the colonial government. Traditionally, many mosques were maintained by the Sultan – not so much as a formally recognised obligation of the state, but rather in accordance with the Sultan's role as the biggest patron of the country.[18] Under British domination, however, rule had been reorganised into a more formalised structure: The Sultan's wealth had been transformed into a state treasury administered by British headed governmental departments. The upkeep of mosques formerly maintained by the Sultan now presented a financial

---

[17] For the features of British administrative policy described here see ZNA, AB 34/1, ZNA, HD 6/55.

[18] See ZNA, AB 34/1.

responsibility of the colonial government. Government officials felt ambivalent about that responsibility. On the one hand, mosque upkeep was a burden on the government's chronically short funds. On the other hand, to reject responsibility for mosques would have been detrimental to the legitimacy of British rule in the eyes of the local public. Waqf presented a welcome solution to this dilemma. Provided that waqf was managed on business lines, it could yield sufficient income to relieve government funds of the burden of mosque upkeep.

There were further interests of the colonial administration which called for British control of charitable waqf. The government had developed a number of "Town Improvement Schemes", which included the building of new roads, new sanitation and various administrative buildings. With a view to these development schemes the colonial administration was eager to gain as much control of urban real estate as possible. Controlling waqf administration proved helpful in this respect. Quite a few development projects were planned on waqf land. On several occasions, the Waqf Commission leased the land in question to the government, and did so on terms that were not "business-like" at all: In most cases the land was leased to the government for ninety-nine years on a merely nominal rent.[19]

From a legal point of view, these leases were questionable. They amounted to the abandonment of resources earmarked for mosque upkeep in order to assist the government in its town improvement schemes. To justify their course of action, the Waqf Commissioners pointed out that according to Islamic law the building of roads, sanitation and other public facilities presented legitimate purposes for religious endowment. This argument, of course, could not do away with the fact that the Waqf Commissioners, by their course of action, violated the express will of the endowments' founders. On the other hand, British officials thought of waqf in terms of "charity", which in turn they understood as synonymous with public benefit of any kind.[20] The Waqf Commissioners no doubt understood that their course of action was dubious from a legal point of

[19] For waqf rented to the government see ZNA, HD 10/34, Secretary to the Waqf Commission to Chief Secretary on 10th of May 1923; HD 3/2, Secretary to the Waqf Commission to Chief Secretary on 12th of April 1915; HD 5/9, Sinclair to Resident on 31st of March 1920 and subsequent correspondence, especially McClellan to Attorney General on 29th of April 1920.

[20] See ZNA, HD 10/34, Secretary to the Waqf Commission to Chief Secretary on 10th of May 1923; HD 10/46, Minute No. 7 of 21st of May 1943.

view. Nonetheless, they deemed their course of action legitimate, as it was in line with British notions of how "charitable" resources should be used.

As regards "family waqf", British controlled management of such endowments did not serve any immediate material interests of the colonial administration. Revenue derived from family waqf was distributed to the stipulated beneficiaries, viz. the founder's offspring. The Waqf Commissioners only retained 5% of those funds as management fees. Thus, from a financial point of view, the business-like administration imposed on family waqf served the interests of the families, not those of the colonial administration. However, business-like management of family waqf had a side effect that probably was quite intended by British officials: In 1897, the British administration had abolished slavery in Zanzibar. British officials had hoped that the freed slaves would turn to wage labour to make a living. However, that hope was largely frustrated. Most freed slaves preferred to stay economically dependent on patrons. They continued to work on their former owner's plantation in exchange for free dwelling on his land and the right to cultivate plots of land for their own subsistence. In other words: The freed slaves turned into clients.[21] The business-like administration of family waqf imposed by the British administration disturbed this mode of subsistence. Occupants of family waqf now had to pay rent, and to afford rent, they had to pick up wage labour. Thus, business-like administration of family waqf put pressure on patrons and clients to turn into wage labourers and entrepreneurs.

Conclusion

On a conceptual level, the history of waqf in Zanzibar can be described as a renegotiation of the normative frame of reference for endowment practice. Part of that frame of reference was, of course Islamic law: Both the traditional political elites as well as the British administration in principle agreed that waqf practice should be governed by that law. Islamic law, however, was not the only frame of reference. It interacted with specific concepts of social order, such as traditional patterns of patronage or, in the case of British waqf administration, mod-

---

[21] The British officials called this practice "squatting". The practice was in fact a continuation of the traditional arrangement to provide for the livelihood of slaves. On squatting see Middleton 1961: 43ff.; Depelchin 1991: 24, 27f. , 29.

ern capitalism with an entrepreneurial bourgeoisie and a class of wage labourers. Those concepts of social order significantly shaped the views of local and colonial agents on how Islamic law should be interpreted and implemented.

The Islamic normative tradition does not prescribe any specific social order. In fact, the manifold Islamic societies that existed (and exist) in the course of time show a considerable diversity in their social structure. Contrary to the influential thesis of Gellner, Islam is not a "blueprint of a social order".[22] On the other hand, Islam can always be interpreted as prescribing a specific social order – be it one already existent or one desired to emerge. The history of waqf in colonial Zanzibar is a case in point. In that history, the interpretation of Islam was renegotiated as a result of a shift in the local constellation of political power. Both the traditional elites of the Sultanate and British officials pointed to their own interpretation of Islamic law. Both interpretations were designed to legitimise a socio-political structure that conformed to specific economic and political interests.

References

Cooper, Frederick (1977): *Plantation Slavery on the East Coast of Africa*. New Haven & London: Heinemann.

Depelchin, Jacques (1991): The Transition from Slavery, 1873-1914. In: Sheriff, Abdul and Ed Fergusson (eds.): *Zanzibar under Colonial Rule*. London, Nairobi, Dar Es Salam & Athens: James Currey, 11-35.

Fair, Laura (2001): *Pastimes and Politics. Culture, Community and Identity in Post-Abolition Urban Zanzibar 1890-1945*. Athens & Oxford: Ohio University Press.

Gellner, Ernest (1981): *Muslim Society*. Cambridge: Cambridge University Press.

Hennigan, Peter C. (2004): *The Birth of a Legal Institution. The Formation of Waqf in the Third-Century A.H. Ḥanafī Legal Discourse*. Leiden and Boston: Brill.

Issa, Amina Ameir (1995): The Burial of the Elite in Nineteenth-Century Zanzibar Stone Town. In: Sheriff, Abdul (ed.): *The History and Conservation of Zanzibar Stone Town*. London: James Currey, 67-80.

[22] See the opening paragraph in Gellner (1981).

Middleton, John (1961): Land Tenure in Zanzibar. *Colonial Research Studies* 33, London: H. M. Stationery Office.

Peters, Rudolph (2002): *Waqf.* In: *Encyclopaedia of Islam* (New Edition), Vol. 9, 59-63.

Pouwels, Randall (1987): *Horn and Crescent. Cultural Changes and Traditional Islam on the East African Coast, 800-1900.* African Studies Series 63. Cambridge: Cambridge University Press.

Sheriff, Abdul (2001): The Records of the "Wakf Commission" as a Source of Social and Religious History of Zanzibar. In: Amoretti, Biancamaria Scarcia (ed.): *Islam in East Africa: New Sources*. Rome: Herder, 27-45.

Z.L.R.: *Zanzibar Law Reports* 8 (1886-1956). Printed and published by the Government Printer, Zanzibar.

ZNA: *Zanzibar National Archives*.

"The Best Interest of the Child": Global Governmentality and Transnational Adoption

Signe Howell

Throughout the twentieth century, the state in Western Europe has increasingly involved itself in organising the private lives of its citizens, manifesting what Foucault has termed governmentality. Michel Foucault argues that the welfare of the population became of increasing concern of the emergent state from the 18th century onwards (1991: 100-101). In a certain sense, the state became the moral guardian of its citizens. As an indirect mechanism of rule by state powers, governmentality is primarily concerned with "the conduct of conduct", that is with the ways in which human conduct is directed by calculated means (Dean 1999, in Gupta 2001: 111). Governmentality has been on the agenda of the "advanced liberal democratic state" (Miller & Rose 1990) for quite some time in most Western European countries and is usually thought about as exercised by national governments, but it may also, I suggest, be discerned to operate on a global scale, especially as it is manifested within the fields of human rights and the ensuing normative edicts and regulations pertaining to the personal and private life of citizens globally. This implies, in effect, a globalisation of Western morality and rationality. The promotion of international policies and legislation to ensure the quality of children's life is a prime example of governmentality on a global scale.

With a particular focus on the practice of transnational adoption, an overall concern in this article will be with questions pertaining to the indirect mechanisms of rule, "those that have enabled, or sought to enable, government at a distance" (Miller & Rose 1990: 83) According to P. Miller and N. Rose, governmentality is dependent upon a number of "technologies of government" that allow for a normalisation of conduct. This not only involves grand concepts like nationhood or the free market, but requires for its success a number of "apparently humble and mundane mechanisms which appear to make it possible to govern: techniques of notation, computation and calculation; procedures of examinations and assessments [...] surveys, statistics [...] professional specialisms [...]" (ibid.1990: 82). Within the field of transnational adoption, it is clear that the liberal (wealthy) democratic nations of Western Europe feel a moral responsibility to ensure that this is conducted according to what they regard as to proper procedure. It is a normative exercise directed at those nations that are less favoured, but who, have the "goods" (the children) so desired by Europeans and North Americans. While the goal is to bring abandoned children to involuntarily childless Western couples, state authorities in receiving countries ensure that they control the transaction – albeit from the best of motives, namely to ensure that the "best interest of the child" is safeguarded and that trafficking children is prevented. Two international conventions: The 1989 UN Convention of the Rights of the Child (CRC), and The Hague Convention on Inter-country Adoption, initiated and largely formulated by Western member countries, exist precisely to ensure that the movement of children in adoption across national boundaries be conducted in a morally acceptable manner and according to a set of rules; rules that they themselves have made and which are based on their values of childhood and family. In order to achieve this, representatives from the Western countries employ a mixture of persuasion and compulsion. With the conventions metaphorically in their hands, Western adoption officials impose conditions before releasing funds or granting legitimacy to local institutions, they monitor practices, they arrange courses and seminars for local staff during which the "technologies of knowledge" are imparted, they flatter and cajole and invite senior government servants and orphanage personnel to visit their own country (all expenses paid). However, from the perspective of many donor countries this attempt at control – however well-intentioned – is viewed with dismay. Many smart under what they feel as paternalistic and neo-colonial attitudes; that the formalities and demands of the transaction are an imposition.

The practice of transnational adoption

Since the late nineteen sixties, transnational adoption has emerged as a global phenomenon. The last thirty years have witnessed a rapid increase in the movement of infants and young children from the poor South (and more recently from the former Soviet bloc) to eagerly awaiting prospective parents in the rich North. Due to a sharp decline in infants being made available for adoption locally, involuntarily childless couples in Western Europe and North America who wish to create a family have to look to the developing world.

An estimated 40,000 children were adopted annually in this manner during the late nineteen-nineties, and the demand is steadily increasing. Adoption – whether domestic or transnational – raises questions concerning the significance attributed to biogenetic relations versus social relations within a lived world of kinship. In order to carry out its duties towards its citizens, an increased state involvement in matters of family life is becoming more and more dependent upon expert knowledge. Adoption has become a practice that is carried out in line with the expertise of a set of professions that derive their knowledge from psychology (social workers, pedagogues, therapists, family lawyers); experts I term psycho-technocrats (Howell 2006a, b). In transnational adoption we may observe a relationship between donors and receivers that is hierarchical and which is perceived by the different partners in very different ways; as generous guidance to ensure "the best interest of the child" by Western countries, as paternalistic and neglectful of local values by donor countries. This raises questions about the nature of the relationship between the North and the South and in this article I shall look at how some countries try to assert a degree of agency in their relationship with the powerful North.

Several levels of relationships are activated in connection with transnational adoption, all of which are informed by law. Each relationship has its own raison d'être and each gives rise to its own set of values and interactions. First, there is the relationship between nation states, acting as agents. Each has its own legal provisions that have to be accommodated before an adoption may be completed. Second, there are the relationships which are informed by international conventions, namely, those between international and national agencies and national bureaucracies and agencies in donor countries. Third, the relationship between adoption agencies in receiving countries and the local institutions that look after children released for adoption overseas. Fourth, the relationship within the receiving country between prospective adoptive parents and the public authorities that decides on their application. In what follows I shall not concern myself with the last relationship.

Legislation in Scandinavia and other European countries on children and adoption and the associated infrastructure, are the manifest expressions of national governmentality. Similarly international conventions and guidelines and the establishment of a global infrastructure to supervise the implementation of these, are the manifest expressions of global governmentality. In both cases, psychologically informed discourses, voiced and managed by the psycho-technocrats who work both nationally and internationally, legitimate practice (Howell 2006a, b). The active involvement of state powers has taken on a global dimension as the so-called international community increasingly involves itself in the internal politics of sovereign states of the South. Children in adoption are moved from the jurisdiction of one country to another; from those less developed economically and technologically in the South to the much wealthier North where there is a growing demand for them. The diffusion of ideas, however, moves in the opposite direction: from the liberal democracies of the economically developed Western nation-states to those that are less developed in the South and in Eastern Europe – but who provide the children so desired by the North. I shall examine this ironical situation from the point of view of a globalisation of Western knowledge, rationality and morality and the reactions to this by some donor countries. To what extent they can exercise any form of agency in their dealings with the countries that receive their children will be an important question. I shall suggest that two ideological concepts, anchored in Western understanding, have emerged as pivotal in the discursive practices of transnational adoption; those of the autonomous individual and the dictum of the best interest of the child. Closely linked to these two are discourses about rights: human rights and children's rights. These do not always find a resonance in many of the donor countries, but the mechanisms of global governmentality that are observable in transnational adoption, are currently transforming childhood itself in so far as, to varying degree, donor countries find themselves helpless and incapable of withstanding the pressure of the humanitarian zeal of representatives from receiving organisations.

The shift in ultimate control over children – from the family to public authorities – that took place in Europe during the second half of the nineteenth century, and was consolidated throughout the twentieth century in legislation, is now happening on a global scale. Global law about children (in the form of international conventions) seeks to ensure the "best interests of the child" by transferring authority not only from the family to the state, but also from the state to the international level. This is very explicit in the case of transnational adoption.

The UN Convention on the Rights of the Child and the more specialised Hague Convention on of Intercountry Adoption both spring out of the UN Declaration on Human Rights (1948), and their prime aims are to safeguard the "best interests of the child". The child is taken to be a universal being and its best interest to be the same everywhere. The initiative for both conventions was taken in Europe, and the principles and values upon which they are formulated derive their impetus from Western values as these are expressed in child, family and adoption laws. The responsibility for overseeing that the conventions are implemented in the various countries that have signed and ratified them is placed in the hands of national public agencies in each country, which carry out their duties under the beady eyes of the West channelled through UNESCO. Furthermore, the locus of control and monitoring of the implementation of the various edicts are located in the West: at UNICEF head-quarters in New York in the case of the UNCRC and in The Hague in the case of the Convention on Inter-country Adoption. The overarching principle of the best interests of the child – never a clear dictum but one that emphasises the importance of being brought up by one's biological parents – has been expanded to emphasise children's rights, agency and empowerment. The so-called "3 Ps" – protection, provision, participation – are, I argue, not only sociocentric and normative, but their meaning has received little debate. At the same time, the globalisation of Western notions of childhood springs out of a genuine desire on the part of the wealthy nations to safeguard and improve the lives of unprotected children.

Adoption to the wealthy counties in Europe and North America, many of whom are previous colonial powers, is a highly sensitive political issue and there is not always consensus within each country regarding the practice. Undoubtedly, all the countries that give up abandoned and orphaned children for adoption to overseas do so because they are unable, or unwilling, to provide for the children themselves. The countries that receive children do so due to an increasing demand from their own citizens who are unable to procreate biologically. All involved experience an ambivalence regarding the practice. Because sending children abroad in adoption manifests an inability to look after one's own abandoned children, many a donor country feels embarrassed about this, and regards it as shameful. Adoption to overseas is therefore a practice that, in many cases, the nation states themselves wish to be seen to control. However, in an attempt to ensure that adoptions are carried out in a manner that is morally and legally acceptable, increasingly the two international conventions superimpose their injunctions upon local practices and the national legal system. Not all developing countries receive the values and rules of the two conventions with equanimity. This will be the focus of the rest of the article.

From the best interest of the child to children's rights and empowerment

A relevant question is whether the category of childhood is general or generalisable. According to Erica Burman, "all too often professionals, activists and policy makers get so caught up in the pain, distress and needs they work with that the answers to these questions are either assumed or dismissed as irrelevant to practice" (Burman 1996: 46). The chairman to the committee that drafted the CRC is quoted as having said that children are the same everywhere and that culture provides only minor varieties. This point is worth bearing in mind when we examine the international treaties which, after all, were drafted in order to protect a category of humanity deemed incapable of protecting itself.

Judith Ennew argues that Western thinking holds strongly that childhood should take place inside a home, inside a family, a private dwelling, and those who do not conform to this literally fall outside – outside society, outside childhood (Ennew 1995: Chapter 15). One of the most provocative issues to many engaged in work in connection with the Year of the Child of 1984 was precisely the street children. They represented the starkest challenge to the Western notion of modern childhood, which, she states, has been globalised through colonialism and later through "the imperialism of international aid" (ibid.: 202, see also Boyden 1997 Chapter 9, Stephens 1995, Burman 1996.) In so far as the two conventions seek to guide the practices not only of legislatures and courts, but also of parents, police, social welfare agencies, health care professionals and others who work with and have responsibility for children, it may be characterised as a tool for effecting state control.

The diversity of cultural understanding receives a nodding acknowledgment at the end of the Preamble of the CRC: "Taking due account of the importance of the traditions and cultural values of each people for the protection and harmonious development of the child". However, the implications of this are not pursued in the actual articles, nor in the subsequent monitoring reports. By making the individual child the basic unit at the expense of an analytic understanding that persons are constituted through the particularity of their sociality – whose meaning in each case is derived from local cultural and social ideas and practices – a conceptual leap is made from the individual to the universal and the global. Culture is rendered epiphenomenal and children are, in effect, desocialised and deculturised.

Discussions on the draft text started at the time when Romania was experiencing major problems in preventing malpractices in the adoption of children to foreign couples. Reports of this in Western European and North American media, coupled with information about appalling conditions in many orphanages and children's homes, soon took on a sensationalist slant. According to Nigel Cantwell (2002: 1), the issues raised by the situation in Romania, and subsequently in Russia and other Eastern European countries, greatly influenced the tone and emphasis of the final texts. A need to establish legally binding standards, and a need for a system of supervision in order to ensure that these standards are observed, were the main reasons for initiating the Convention (Parra Aranguren 1994: 179).

The unquestioned supreme status of the individual in the conventions is contested. Both capitalist and communist ideologies regard kinned relatedness as unimportant; the former to the supremacy of the individual, the latter to that of the community. This is not the case in many countries in Africa, Asia and Latin America from which Western nations adopt children. Most do not share in the belief of the supremacy of the autonomous individual, but perceive personhood and community as being constituted through relations. Kinship becomes a determining factor for significant relatedness, but kinship need not necessarily be predicated upon biological connectedness. It is the social and emotional process of kinning that creates kinship – not biology.

Despite the many objections that were voiced by non-Western country representatives during the drafting of the two conventions (Howell 2006), most nation states ended up signing and ratifying them. However, some alternative conventions have been formulated by countries in the South in order to circumvent particularly objectionable sections in global conventions. One such is the African Charter on the Rights and Welfare of the Child.

The African Charter on the Rights and Welfare of the Child

Reservations voiced by some African countries during the drafting of the UNCRC resulted in a charter that was intended to give voice to African values and to contrast them to some of the CRC. One African commentator criticises what he calls the Western "[…] obsessive, concern with the dignity of the individual, his worth, personal autonomy and property". The Organization of African Unity agreed in 1990 on the formulation of The African Charter on the Rights of the Child (ACRWC). For a discussion of the background to the Charter, see Olusola Ojo 1990. It is a document that I interpret as an act of resistance against what is perceived as attempted imposition of Western values. The Charter starts by affirming its adherence to the CRC, but also to The African Charter on Human and Peoples Rights. It does not diverge from most of the paragraphs of the CRC, but makes a strong argument for the need to take account of African practices and values and to regard children as integral members of their communities, not as isolated individuals.

While the CRC employs the language of universality, the African critics insist that it frequently expresses values and assumptions directly attributable to a contemporary Western view. In order to balance this trend and to make the provisions more in line with "African values and practices", the Preamble states: "Taking into consideration the virtues of their cultural heritage, historical background and the values of the African civilisation (sic) which should inspire and characterise their reflection on the concept of the rights and welfare of the child […]". And making the point that rights should not be isolated from responsibilities, they continue, "[c]onsidering that the promotion and protection of the rights and welfare of the child also implies the performance of duties on the part of everyone".

The Africans are critical of what they regard as the failure of the CRC to perceive children as constituted as persons through their relationship with others: their parents and members of the wider kin group. In order to balance the emphasis upon the rights of the child, the Charter places these within a discourse of obligations and duties. For example, Article 31, entitled "Responsibility of the Child", states:

> "Every child shall have duties towards his family and society, the State and other legally recognised communities and the international community. The child [...] shall have the duty:
>
> (a) to work for the cohesion of the family, to respect his parents, superiors and elders at all times and to assist them in case of need;
> (b) to serve the national community by placing his physical and intellectual abilities at its service:
> (c) to preserve and strengthen social and national solidarity;
> (d) to preserve and strengthen their independence and the integrity of his country;
> (e) to contribute to the best of his abilities, at all times, and at all levels, to the promotion and achievement of African Unity."

These provisions are very different indeed from those contained in both the Declaration of Human Rights and the CRC. As such, they demonstrate attempts to resist global (Euro-American) enforcement of ideas and values concerning family, kinship and personhood. According to Ojo "[t]he main distinguishing features of the charter are the concept of and emphasis on people's rights as opposed to individual rights and the importance attached to 'duties' as opposed to 'rights'" (Ojo 1999: 119).

Global governmentality and donor countries: some reactions from donor countries

I now want to follow up on this and consider the reaction to the Conventions and to the procedures that these have given rise to in countries that send children to the West for adoption. What I am interested in eliciting is the methods they employ to assert themselves (or not) against this ideological onslaught, from open resistance through the employment of a variety of the "weapons of the weak", subtle alterations, to almost complete acquiescence. I have studied five donor countries: South Korea, India, Ethiopia, China and Romania. It is clear that the reaction of each country is far from identical, but that, nevertheless, the authorities in each display unease with the practice. Due to the focus of this conference, I will confine myself to Ethiopia.

Ethiopia

Ethiopia is extremely poor with minimal infrastructure and has been torn apart by civil wars and famine for several decades. Given these facts, the room for manoeuvre by the state is limited. Most commentators, whether local or foreign, agree that Ethiopia would barely survive as a modern nation-state were it not for the foreign aid that the country receives. Accompanying the aid are normative values. In recent years, a large section of foreign aid has been directed at children and the plight of women. In such a cultural setting, where mere survival requires supreme efforts, the notion of children's rights has not been met with much understanding from the authorities (Berre 2004).

Transnational adoption began in the early nineteen-seventies when thousands of children were orphaned or abandoned as a result of drought, famine and severe and prolonged civil wars. The first orphanages were established at this time by the government and by foreign NGOs and missionaries. More recently, the explosive spread of HIV/AIDS in Ethiopia has led to thousands more children being orphaned. This renders the country extremely vulnerable and, in the words of a prominent journalist who I interviewed, "what poverty does is to discourage debate about Western values being imposed". Similar sentiments were expressed by a senior officer at the government office handling child care and adoption (MOLSA). He told me that most issues that he had to deal with in his work emanated from Western donor concerns and values. Like the journalist, he said that the Western concern with the value of the individual and the nuclear family in development projects were not very relevant in the Ethiopian context. The fact that both the CRC and the Hague Convention base their recommendations upon the centrality of the individual child and the nuclear family, makes it difficult for Ethiopians to continue to adhere to traditional values. He nevertheless insisted that the underlying premises of the conventions are shared and that the objectives are good. He added that Western targets for development are very idealistic, especially the stress that is continually placed on the best interest of the child, the meaning of which Ethiopians sometimes find difficult to understand. He was not going to disagree, however, since the resources of the Ethiopian government are very limited and, without the assistance they receive from the West, the situation in the country would be much worse. At the same time, people will continue to practise as they have done for generations, and do whatever is "suitable to our continent" he concluded – i.e. they employ "the weapons of the weak".

There is little doubt that the idea of the autonomous individual and his or her rights is a major stumbling block for meaningful communication. In a critical article entitled "On the rights of the child", M. Retta, an Ethiopian lawyer who works for the Juvenile Justice Project Office in Addis Ababa, considers the position of the many street children in Ethiopia and how they best may be helped by the authorities. He poses the question whether the Ethiopians and non-Ethiopians who are engaged in development work in the country share the same understandings when they speak of the rights of children. His answer is that they probably do not, and he insists that the Ethiopians must not allow themselves to be brow-beaten into accepting what, after all, are values and notions more suited to the rich countries in Europe and North America. "Unlike the child in a rich society who undergoes the 'luxury of identity crisis', more often than not, whenever an Ethiopian child in a poor family demonstrates delinquent behaviour…the motive is clear – it is poverty" (2001: 29). He argues for an acceptance of "indigenous solutions […] rather than imitate or import prescription" (ibid.). He even questions the relevance of the basic principles and regulations of the CRC and other international conventions. To his own question "[a]re the best interests of the Ethiopian and the British and the American child the same?" he replies that institutions and legal provisions that are designed elsewhere are not necessarily suited for Ethiopia. Whereas Retta is outspoken, others may be more cautious, but do not necessarily disagree with his resentment of the rich and powerful nations and organisations which, he says, think that poor nations are "necessarily backward and inferior [and hence] need to do a lot of 'awareness raising' endeavours" (ibid: 10).

Because of poverty, AIDS, and poor infrastructure, the Ethiopian state does not have much room to manoeuvre. Expert knowledge is represented mainly by foreigners working on specific aid projects, and in so far as one may talk of governmentality in the country, this is primarily exercised by the foreigners, not by the Ethiopian state apparatus. Senior public servants may sometimes be resentful but, realising their impotence, most are also pragmatic.

A somewhat different approach was observed in 2006 in Malawi when the American film star Madonna tried to adopt a Malawian boy from a local state-run orphanage. This provoked strong reaction inside the country which then caught the attention of the international media. The Malawian Human Rights Consultative Committee made up of 67 organisations alleged that Madonna had acted against Malawian adoption law which holds that a foreign adoptive parent must reside in the country for a certain length of time before the child may be taken abroad. They insisted on a court hearing which kept being postponed and Madonna was allowed to bring the boy to England on a temporary permit until it could be resolved. The Malawian reaction may be interpreted as an ideological resistance against foreigners attempting to override local legislation ... Commenting on the case in the Weekly Forum for Social Justice in Africa, a journalist argues that the reason for the resistance can be found in a perceived imbalance in the regulations about transnational adoption. In so far as they provide only for adopters being in the rich West, he argues, "[…] there appears to be no provisions for wealthy Malawians […] to adopt and take a child out of England. For some, this imperial-Empire axis of the relationship is one of the mains sources of their disquiet" (Bing-Pappoe 2006: 4).

Conclusion

It is important to remember that transnational adoption is not development aid. It is a transaction that directly benefits citizens of both nations states involved in any one transaction. Nevertheless, due to the fact that the directives of the two international conventions are formulated on the basis of contemporary Western understating of the best interest of the child, it is not a balanced relationship. What has emerged in my study of transnational adoption as a global phenomenon is that the practice gives rise to a number of ambivalent emotional, intellectual and political reactions on part of the donor countries. These can, I suggest, be linked to the general political and ideological discourse that arose in the aftermath of post-colonialism and which shows overtones of paternalism. At the same time, as the notion about the state's responsibility towards the welfare of its citizens became an established truth in the North, in today's politico-economic situation this entails a globalisation of Western morality and rationality.

References

Berre, Kjersti (2004): *„For when the Guests Come": The Introduction of Child Participation in Northern Ethiopia.* VDM Verlag Dr. Müller

Bing-Pappoe, Adotey (2006): David and Madonna. *Pambazuka News: Weekly Forum for Social Justice in Africa*, 10 November 2006.

Boyden, Jo (1997): Childhood and the Policy Makers: A Comparative Perspective on the Globalisation of Childhood. In: James, Allison and Alan Prout (eds.): *Constructing and Reconstructing Childhood.* London: Falmer Press.

Burman, Erica (1996): Local, Global or Globalised? Child Development and International Child Rights Legislation. *Childhood* 3, 45-66.

Cantwell, Nigel (2002): *The International Scenario – The Hague Convention on Intern-Country Adoption.* Paper presented to the Indian Council for Child Welfare International Convention on Adoption, New Delhi.

Ennew, Judith (1995): Outside Childhood. In: Franklin, Bob (ed.): *The Handbook of Children's Rights.* London: Routledge.

Foucault, Michel (1991): Governmentality. In: Burchell, Graham, Colin Gordon and Peter Miller (eds.): *The Foucault Effect: Studies in Governmentality.* London: Harvester Press, 87-104.

Gupta, Akhil (2001): Governing Populations: The Integrated Child Development Services Program in India. In: Blom-Hansen, Thomas Blom and Finn Stepputat (eds.): *States of Imagination: Ethnographic Explorations of the Postcolonial State.* Durham: Duke University Press.

Howell, Signe (2003): The Diffusion of Moral Values in a Global Perspective. In: Hylland Eriksen, Thomas (ed.): *Transnational Flow of Concepts and Substances: Methodological Issues.* London: Pluto Press.

— (2006a): *The Kinning of Foreigners: Transnational Adoption in a Global Perspective.* Oxford & New York: Berghahn Books.

— (2006b): Changes in Moral Values about the Family: Adoption Legislation in Norway and the US. *Social Analysis* 50 (3), 146-163.

Miller, P. and N. Rose (1990): Governing Economic Life. In: *Economy and Society* February 1990, 1-31.

Parra Aranguren, G. (1994): *Explanatory Report on the 1993 Hague Intercountry Adoption Convention.* The Hague: Proceedings of the Seventeenth Session (1993) Tome II: Adoption.

Ojo, Olusola (1990): Understanding Human Rights in Africa. In: Berting, Jan, Peter R. Baehr et al. (eds.): *Human Rights in a Pluralistic World: Individuals and Collectivities*. London: Meckler Westport.

Retta, M. (2001): On the Rights of the Child. Addis Ababa: *The Federal Supreme Court Juvenile Justice Programme* 1, 1-9.

Rose, Nikolas (1999): *Governing the Soul: the Shaping of the Private Self*. London: Free Association Books.

Stephens, Sharon (ed.) (1995): *Children and the Politics of Culture*. Princeton: Princeton University Press.

Law and Development in Africa: A Changing Legal Programme?

Harald Sippel and Ulrike Wanitzek

Introduction[1]

The "law and development" programme that underlies a large number of legal assistance projects for developing and transition countries worldwide, including Africa, has been the subject of academic work in various legal fields.[2] The concept of "law and development" was created and reflected on by academics as a legal programme to support the social and economic progress of a country by suitable legal measures. In the 1960s, when numerous African countries were released into independence by the colonial powers, "law and development" became an intensively discussed topic in relation to the legal systems of developing countries. It was based on the modernisation theory. In the following decade, however, it was confronted, among other things, with reproaches of "Euro- (and US-America-) centrism" and "legal imperialism" and soon lost much of its academic significance. With the collapse of the Soviet Union, the programme received new attention in the 1990s, not only for the successor states of the Soviet Union and other transition countries in Eastern Europe, but also for developing countries in Africa, Asia and Latin America. This renewed approach connected "law and development" with demands for the observance of democracy and human rights, as well as principles of good governance and the market economy. "Law and development" can thus be described as a case of "changing world views".

---

1 This article is based on a paper presented on 26 April 2007 at the Symposium on Agency and Changing World views in Africa held by the research centre SFB/FK 560 at the University of Bayreuth, Germany. The case study presented here and the literature evaluated for this paper represent the position as of 2007, apart from a literature update undertaken for this publication.

2 See for instance the articles in the Law and Development Review (<http: //www. bepress.com/ldr/>). For a critical analysis of some recently published, mainly American literature on the concept of law and development, see Davis & Trebilcock 2008. A four-volume publication containing a large number of basic texts within the field of law and development is being prepared (Faundez, forthcoming 2012).

The change from views influenced by modernisation theory to those developed under the influence of globalisation will be the subject of the first part of this article. Its second part provides a discussion on whether the change of world views underlying the programme of "law and development" really meant a change in the substance and effects of the programme. This requires an investigation into the local effects of the programme and the ways in which local actors deal with them. This question will be discussed on the basis of a recent case in the field of land law, one of the major areas in which "law and development" programmes have been promoted.

Changing world views

The roots of "law and development" in the colonial period

The origins of the "law and development" programme can be traced back to the colonial period in the 20th century. According to Anthony Carty (1992: xi), the French university discipline droit du développement "grew quite openly out of colonial law and the law of cooperation in the period preceding the independence of the French colonies". While the legal activities of the European colonial powers, which were mainly in the field of administrative law, were indeed meant to "develop" their colonial territories within the colonial understanding of development bearing mainly their own political and economic interests in mind, this was not based on any thought-out legal concept or programme of law as an instrument to bring about social change and development (Bryde 1986: 11).

The first wave of "law and development" in the 1960s and 1970s

When a large number of previous colonial territories became politically independent in the early 1960s, they were considered to be "underdeveloped" by Western standards, "lacking, among other things, unity and modernity in their legal systems. Western societies were viewed as possessing the models and the know-how for raising up the underdeveloped states in Latin America, Africa and Asia […]" (Burg 1977: 495). On the basis of this assumption, Western actors in the field of development aid, as well as academics, worked out a programme of "law and development", a major supposition of which was that the transfer of laws from the "developed" to the "underdeveloped"[3] countries and

[3] Bryde (1986: 13) notes that "strange" legal elements (i.e. elements unknown to the Western jurists) were often quickly declared to be symptoms of "underdevelopment".

the implementation of these laws in those countries would contribute to their development. This was seen as the "modernisation of law".[4]

Considerable criticism of, and resistance against, this shaping of the "law and development" programme arose in the 1970s, to a large extent from within the "law and development" movement itself, by some of the major proponents of the programme, such as Marc Galanter (Galanter & Trubek 1974). It was criticised that the programme was too Western-oriented and did not take into account the cultural, social and political contexts of the receiving countries within which the transferred laws were to be applied. The programme was further criticised because of the legal imperialism which it represented, for any implementation of the transferred Western laws must include implementation of the Western values contained in these laws (Merryman 1977: 479; Burg 1977: 517). It was noted critically that the political framework of the law was ignored, and that law was viewed as a tool to achieve development without taking note of the political context (Bryde 1986: 14). For instance, it was often assumed that the goals were clear and that it was therefore sufficient to develop the legal instruments to achieve these goals, while in fact there was no political consensus regarding the goals (Bryde 1986: 14). On the other hand it was assumed that the new laws would be fully implemented, which was, in Brun-Otto Bryde's words, "an idealistic over-estimation of the role of the state in the third world".[5] In reality, many laws transferred from European states to African states existed only in the statute books of the latter but were irrelevant in legal reality (Allott 1980: 6). Moreover, the danger was seen that within the law and development programme "too much law" would be created in certain cases, and that this over-regulation would worsen rather than improve the situation in the developing countries (Burg 1977: 517, 518). It was also criticised that there was no real theory regarding the relationship between law and the economic and political development of a country (Trubek 2001: 8443). Since at that time "law and development" programmes originated mainly from the United States, the controversial debates in the 1970s and 1980s were mostly related to the transfer of US-American values, through US-American law, to developing countries. This "can be regarded as an internal American disagreement which should not be allowed

[4] This was the title of Galanter's legal contribution to a volume on modernisation (Galanter 1966).

[5] Bryde 1986: 14 (translated from the German original).

to dominate the problematic of law and development as such" (Carty 1992: xi; Merryman 1977: 479). As a consequence, the "law and development" programme disappeared from the academic agenda in the USA (Trubek 2001: 8444), but not necessarily in other countries such as France and Great Britain (Tamanaha 1995: 474).[6] Supported by foreign donor organisations, African countries continued to reform their laws in various ways in the name of "law and development".

The rediscovery of "law and development" in the 1990s

The "law and development" programme was rediscovered in academic circles at the beginning of the 1990s when, at the end of the cold war, a new need for "development" arose in the former Soviet Union and in Eastern European and Asian transition states (Trubek 2001: 8444). At the same time there was a new wave of law-focussed development projects in the developing countries of the South generally.

According to Franz von Benda-Beckmann (2006: 53, 54), an important starting point for this new development was the World Bank's re-interpretation of its statutes. Until then, the Bank had had no mandate to interfere in the political and administrative organisation of the countries with which it cooperated, and it could only prescribe "economic" considerations as criteria for decision taking. Now, however, the meaning of "economic" was re-interpreted, changing the previous understanding of politics and law as external factors to an acceptance of them as factors relevant to economic growth. "For instance, the definition and protection of property rights, the creation of an effective judicial system, and later 'good governance', became relevant factors for a healthy economy" (von Benda-Beckmann 2006: 54). This new policy was expressed in the World Development Report of 1991 in the following words: by "defining and protecting property rights; providing effective legal, judicial, and regulatory systems; improving the efficiency of the civil service and probably the environment, the state forms the very core of development."[7] As Franz von Benda-Beckmann (2006: 54) puts it: "This shift contributed to the new boom in law and development activities."

---

[6] In Germany the whole debate took place largely unnoticed (Bryde 1986: 14).

[7] Cited according to von Benda-Beckmann 2006: 54.

Forces on two levels were, and continue to be, relevant in this renewed, second wave of "law and development", i.e. the legal and the economic levels (Trubek 2001: 8444): On the legal level, this included the principles of democratisation, the rule of law and human rights; and on the economic level, the liberalisation of the economy and the establishment and strengthening of the market economy. Usually, both levels are combined with each other, for instance in land law: the protection of property as a human right on the one hand, and the market economy on the other.

The role of the state also changed under the renewed "law and development" programme. According to the renewed programme, the state has a more passive role than it was supposed to have under projects of the first wave of the "law and development" programme, while more autonomy is now granted to private individuals than was the case under the former programme (Trubek 2001: 8444). The state no longer plays the role of the "developer" under the new programme, and room for a more autonomous development is granted to the population, which means, according to Ambreena Manji, a shift from the "developmental state" to the "neoliberal state in [the] age of globalisation" (2005: 123).

Following this overview of the successive waves of the "law and development" programme, the question arises whether any substantial changes in the programme can be identified between the first and second waves, and particularly whether any lessons have been learnt from the criticisms of the first wave; could it be that the programme has been modified only with regard to minor aspects, while remaining unchanged in its central aspects? These questions can best be addressed by looking at them from the local perspective, because some of the major criticisms referred to the failure to take into account local political, social, cultural and economic conditions (Davis & Trebilcock 2008: 932-938). Therefore it is necessary to examine local agency in Africa in respect of legal projects conducted under the "law and development" programme.

Local agency

The case of Sinya village, Tanzania

An example may be useful to illustrate this question.[8] The following events took place in Tanzania, East Africa, nearly six years after the Tanzanian Land Act and Village Land Act of 1999 had entered into force in mid-2001. These two Acts were the final product of a process of land law reform in Tanzania that lasted more than ten years (Juma, Sippel and Wanitzek 2004: 231-238). The specific objectives of the Tanzanian National Land Policy of 1995 included to "ensure that land is put to its most productive use to promote rapid social and economic development in the country" (United Republic of Tanzania 1997: 5). It seemed apt to choose an example from the field of land law since, as Patrick McAuslan puts it, "[t]here are few more important aspects to the life of any society than land and the relations between land and human kind" (2003: 3).

On 16th April 2007 the Tanzanian newspaper "The Guardian" reported on a case concerning Sinya village.[9] This is a Maasai pastoralist community of 828 inhabitants in Arusha Region, Monduli District, and Longido Ward, in the north of Tanzania, west of Mount Kilimanjaro and close to the Kenyan border. The village had entered into a ten-year lease agreement with a tourist company[10] specialised in wildlife tourism. According to the agreement, the tourist company would occupy 45,000 acres or 182 km² of village land for the purpose of tourist activities.[11] The village would earn 3,500 US-Dollars annually as every tourist visiting the site was to pay 10 US-Dollars per day. The deal was approved without any objection by the Sinya village assembly at two meetings which were attended by 33 and 70 villagers respectively. The agreement was duly signed by both parties.

---

8 The authors acknowledge Dr Kennedy Gastorn's assistance in kindly drawing their attention to the following case. The larger context of the case is described, among others, in Nelson 2007: 105-121, 114; Trench et al. 2009: 217 ff., 245 ff.; Sulle et al. 2011: 11 ff.; Benjaminsen et al. 2011: 6 f.

9 <http://www.ippmedia.com/ipp/guardian/2007/04/16/88531.html>; see Gastorn 2008: 75-76.

10 Tarangire River Camp. On an earlier agreement concluded in 2001 with another tourism company, Kibo Safaris, for high-paying clients, see Honey 2008: 215.

11 1 acre = 4,046.8 m²; 45,000 acres = 182,106 km² which is equivalent to the size of a square with sides of 13.5 km each.

When the District Commissioner[12] heard about the agreement, he visited the village at once, intervened and demanded the immediate cancellation of the agreement. He told the Sinya village representatives that the agreement was null and void because the village authority had no mandate to give 45,000 acres away without seeking the authorisation of the Commissioner for Lands in writing.[13] The District Commissioner also asked why those villagers who had signed the agreement were taken for a sponsored tour to the city of Dar es Salaam with per diems paid to each of them by the tourist company.

According to the press, all villagers who had attended the meetings openly rejected the request of the District Commissioner to terminate the contract with immediate effect. They did, however, indicate that they were ready to discuss and identify the inadequacies of the agreement, if any, and make sure that all legal formalities were observed. To them, the reaction of the district authority was outrageous and blew the matter out of all proportion.

At this stage, as the Guardian further reports, the District Commissioner ordered the arrest of the entire village leadership because of their unilateral decision to sign an agreement in land matters with a tourist company, regardless of the provisions of the Village Land Act and without involving the district authorities. In reaction to this, allegedly hundreds of villagers took part in a peaceful march to Longido central police station to express their anger over the action which was unacceptable to them. The District Commissioner insisted that the central government had directed him to act decisively, and therefore the agreement must be dropped and then cross-checked, because some individuals had taken advantage of the villagers' ignorance of the legal position.

---

12 Mr. James Ole Millya.

13 He further stated that Sinya village did not have the blessing of the village general meeting because the meetings which claimed to have approved the deal did not constitute a quorum in the village which had 828 inhabitants. However, the Local Governments (District Authorities) Act 7/1982 (Cap 287 R.E. 2002), which was referred to, is silent on the question of what constitutes a quorum at village assemblies; see section 105 of Act 7/1982 which provides only that the quorum at any meeting of the village council shall not be less than half of all members of the council; see Gastorn 2008: 76.

Tanzanian land law

It is necessary at this point to examine the applicable legal provisions[14] in order to establish whether the lease agreement between Sinya village and the tourist company was valid or not. Sec. 32 Village Land Act 1999 (VLA)[15] regulates the grant of a lease over village land to a third party by a village. Under this section, an application for grant of a derivative right, which includes a lease,[16] must be made to the village council on a prescribed form, and the village members must be notified by some form of publicity that will bring the matter to their attention.[17]

An application for the grant of a lease is called a "class C" application if it is made for more than ten years, which is not the case here, or if it relates to an area of more than 30 hectares, which is the case here, because the area to be leased consisted of about 18,000 hectares.[18] A "class C" application is determined by the village council subject to approval by the village assembly, and the advice (*ushauri*) of the Commissioner.[19] If the lease has been granted by the village council to the applicant without having received the Commissioner's counter-signature (*sahihi*),[20] as was the case here, the grant of the lease is void (*batili*).[21]

The questions arise whether and how the villagers understood these and other related legal provisions governing village land law in Tanzania.[22] The Acts were drafted by the British consultant, Professor Patrick McAuslan, who was sponsored by the British Overseas Development Agency (ODA), now the

---

14 For details of the major provisions of the Land Act and Village Land Act of 1999, see Juma, Sippel and Wanitzek 2004: 240-249.

15 More exactly: Section 32 (5) (c) and 32 (6) (c) VLA.

16 A lease is a derivative right according to sec 2 VLA.

17 Sec. 32 (2) (a), (e) VLA.

18 More exactly 18,210.5 ha, which is the equivalent of 45,000 acres. 1 ha = 2.4711 acres.

19 Sec. 32 (5) (c) VLA.

20 First the application must be submitted to the Commissioner according to Sec. 32 (6) (c) (iv) VLA.

21 Sec. 32 (9) (d) VLA. Sec. 32 VLA contains some more details which have been omitted here.

22 As already mentioned, the Land Act and Village Land Act of 1999 (Acts 4/1999 and 5/1999, Cap 113 and 114 R.E. 2002, respectively; they must be read together with the Local Government Laws, such as the Local Governments (District Authorities) Act of 1982, see above fn. 11, which were enacted with the goal of bringing about social and economic development, section 3 (1) Land Act, 1999; section 3 (1) Village Land Act, 1998; United Republic of Tanzania 1997, 5.

Department for International Development (DFID). The two Land Acts are voluminous, comprising 186 and 66 sections respectively (i.e. a total of 252 sections). Many of these sections are very detailed and use the typical legal language of English statutes, often with extremely long and complicated sentences. A translation of the Acts into Kiswahili, the national language of Tanzania, exists in the case of the Village Land Act (Sheria ya Ardhi ya Vijiji), but it was published only several years after the Acts had entered into force. Of the extensive subsidiary legislation,[23] which contains further provisions for the application of the Acts in practice (such as forms and procedural regulations), the Village Land Regulations 2001 are another example where there is a translation into Kiswahili (Kanuni za Ardhi ya Vijiji).

Since the Acts and the subsidiary legislation[24] provide for complex procedures to be followed for various activities relating to rights over land, training is required in order to understand them. Although some training of various village and district officers took place, and a training manual and other materials were produced,[25] the level of information provided on those occasions and by these materials remains very general, while the intricacies of the provisions are usually not taught.[26] It can therefore be assumed that in the case of Sinya village the villagers had no full knowledge and understanding of the legal position and therefore acted according to their own local procedures and understandings.

---

23 Subsidiary Legislation to the Gazette of the United Republic of Tanzania No. 18, Vol. 82, dated 4th May, 2001 (Supplement No. 16).

24 The villages are supposed to apply the Land Acts, but not all of them have access to a copy of these statutes and the subsidiary legislation. According to a report by the Permanent Secretary of the Ministry of Lands dated March 2005, the Land Acts and the relevant forms have been distributed to all regions, but only to some districts and villages, Land Symposium Report 2005, 1. In the case of Sinya village, it is not clear whether the texts of the relevant Acts and Regulations had been made available to the village, but it is likely that this was the case because Arusha region was among the regions which were supplied with the texts. It is also known in respect of two neighbouring wards/districts that they were supplied with the Kiswahili version of the Village Land Regulations, information received from Kennedy Gastorn, April 2007.

25 Land Symposium Report 2005: 1.

26 Information received from Kennedy Gastorn, April 2007.

The local context of legal pluralism

The local context for the application of the new land laws is characterised by legal pluralism. Most African states have systems involving legal pluralism.[27] This means that state law recognises African customary laws and religious laws to a certain extent. However, it is not only the official legal pluralism within the state legal system that is relevant for our purposes, but also unofficial forms of legal pluralism which include customary, religious and other local laws that function outside the realm of state law as the living law of the people.[28] Law reform by state legislation must be seen within this unofficial legal pluralistic context. This means that the new laws interact with customary laws, religious laws, or any other local laws of different origins which exist at the place under consideration. This context of law reform is often overlooked in the legal literature on "law and development" where the focus is on the reformed statute as such but not on the pluralistic local context in which it is to be applied.

There is a further component of non-state legal pluralism which must be taken into consideration if it is desired to gain a full picture of law reform within "law and development" programmes. Additional norms exist which determine the actors' interactions and behaviour beyond state law and beyond a certain locality. These are the norms which govern interactions between the whole chain of actors taking part in development projects, such as members and employees of the donor organisations, the local partner organisations, local authorities, the local target groups, the national Ministries, and others (Weilenmann 2005: 131-133). Such norms have been called "project law", and they also contribute to unofficial legal pluralism, besides the local laws referred to above.

In the case under consideration, the local Maasai community of Sinya village had their own ways of handling land matters. The question is whether sec. 32 VLA could have been drafted in a more flexible way so that it could be better adapted to the local conditions. The relevance of the size of the land depends on its usability. So it is questionable why the lease of a relatively small area of 30 hectares should be subject under any circumstances, not depending on its usability, to a complicated procedure involving the consent of the Commissioner

---

[27] On the implications of pluralist concepts of land ownership for development, see Akuffo 2009: 57-78; Alden Wily 2011:733-757.

[28] See Woodman 1998: 21-59 for the debate on the concept of legal pluralism. On the Tanzanian context of land law, see Sippel & Wanitzek 2004: 232.

for Land. The political question involved is to what extent a village should be granted autonomy by the law, and whether a level of autonomy higher than that granted in sec. 32 VLA would not lead to more responsible action by the village representatives.

Also of interest are the norms governing the interactions between Sinya village, the district authority, the Commissioner for Lands, other relevant authorities such as the wildlife authorities, non-governmental organisations active in the area such as Sand County Foundation Community Based Conservation Network, Swedish International Development Cooperation Agency (SIDA), Oxfam and other organisations which hold land law related workshops in the villages, private companies which are active in the area such as the tourist company with which the lease agreement was made, etc. Sec. 32 VLA is thus applicable within a whole network of norms which influence the action of the parties concerned and which should therefore not be ignored, for otherwise the picture would not be complete.

In the legal literature on "law and development", however, these forms of local legal pluralism have not been taken into account by many authors.[29] In the practice of development cooperation, there is growing insight into the relevance of legal pluralism without limiting it to state law exclusively (von Benda-Beckmann 2006: 57)[30] – the insight that plural legal conditions should always be seen as a potentially significant factor of development. Whether legal pluralism is recognised by the state or not, de facto existing local laws may have positive or negative effects on law and development projects. In a situation of legal pluralism it is not possible to analyse any partial legal order, such as state law, in isolation from the other legal orders because people's actions may be influenced by any of the partial legal orders (von Benda-Beckmann 2006: 63).

If legal pluralism is neglected in a "law and development" project, the success of the project is at risk. If law is to bring about development, it will not suffice that new rights exist in the statute book only. According to Amartya Sen,

---

[29] Von Benda-Beckmann 2006: 57 mentions the examples of Seidman, Seidman & Wälde 1998; Nelken & Feest 2001; Hatchard & Perry-Kessaris 2003. Similarly in the literature on law and globalisation, ibid. John notes that customary laws should be seen as a potential for development but that they are not sufficiently known (1998: 278-279).

[30] Examples are the areas of natural resources (including land law) and the rights of indigenous peoples, von Benda-Beckmann 2006: 58 fn. 24, with examples of development organisations.

"this may look like a legal development, and in a sense it clearly is that"; however, if the focus of legal development is to give people rights that they can exercise, then "this putative legal development may be constitutively hollow if [people] do not manage in fact to exercise any of these rights ..."[31] This means that legal "development" is achieved only when people have the capability and freedom to exercise the new rights and entitlements contained in the reformed statute (Sen 2006: 39). And this depends to a high degree on the local legal pluralistic conditions (Pande & Udry 2005: 14-16).

Conclusion

In the context of globalisation, changing world views can be traced within programmes of law and development in the field of land law, where such programmes have been used as instruments to provide developing countries with legal provisions in order to define and secure land rights, with the goal of furthering the development of the country. However, the changes seem to exist more on the surface than in the substance of the reform programmes. In the light of the case of Sinya village in Tanzania (and other comparable cases), it appears that the new wave of "law and development" is not less Eurocentric than the first wave.[32] The new Tanzanian Land Acts were drafted without taking local forms of legal pluralism into account.[33] An overemphasis on the technical aspects of law reform is still visible, connected with a belief in the transferability of foreign law, as well as underestimation of the specific cultural, economic, political and social context at each locality in which the new law is to function (von Benda-Beckmann/von Benda-Beckmann 1999: 23 ff.). The models introduced continue to be too simple on the one hand, because they do not take sufficient notice of the specific local conditions of the place at which the new laws are to be applied (Trubek 2001: 8445, 8446); and on the other hand they continue to be too complicated and too bureaucratic, following Western patterns of highly developed bureaucratic structures, and ignoring existing local mechanisms of finding solutions. As Volkmar Gessner puts it, "The assumption is that

---

31 "The very idea of legal development may then be ... contingent on certain social or economic [or cultural] characteristics", Sen 2006: 39.

32 See also Trubek 2001: 8445; Nader 2006: 99.

33 As for the aspect of security of land tenure in Tanzania within this context, see Juma, Sippel and Wanitzek 2004: 294-304; Sippel & Wanitzek 2004; Wanitzek 2005.

the setting up of an 'adequate' (Western) legal system including legal education and an efficient court structure is a precondition for rapid social and economic change. … Experience shows, however, that success is very limited and that the models have had at most a modest and incremental impact." (Gessner 2001: 8495).[34] It is cumbersome to go to the villages and find out how people handle their land matters locally. But this would add a worthwhile component to law and development programmes, and help to make them more open for the local agency of people under local conditions of legal pluralism. The success of law reform under law and development programmes depends on acceptance of the new law by the local population. This can be achieved only if all existing laws, including unofficial laws, which govern the field of law under consideration, are taken into account.

References

Akuffo, Kwame (2009): The Conception of Land Ownership in African Customary Law and Its Implications for Development. *African Journal of International and Comparative Law* 17, 57-78.

Alden Wily, Liz (2011): 'The Law is to Blame'. The Vulnerable Status of Common Property Rights in Sub-Saharan Africa. *Development and Change* 42, 733-757. Available online: <http://www.onlinelibrary.wiley.com/doi/10.1111/j.1467-7660. 2011.01712.x/pdf>.

Allott, Antony (1980): The Past and Future Contribution of Law to Development in Africa. *Jahrbuch für afrikanisches Recht* 1, 3-19.

Benda-Beckmann, Franz von (2006): The Multiple Edges of Law: Dealing with Legal Pluralism in Development Practice. *World Bank Legal Review: Law, Equity and Development* 2, 51-85.

Benda-Beckmann, Franz von and Keebet von Benda-Beckmann (1999): A Functional Analysis of Property Rights, with Special Reference to Indonesia. In: van Meijl, Toon and Franz von Benda-Beckmann (eds.): *Property Rights and Economic Development. Land and Natural Resources in South-*

[34] "In Latin America as well as in Eastern Europe, law and development programmes [even] proved to be counterproductive, leading to greater class differences, to distorted markets due to monopolistic structures, and to legal cultural rejection of imported models", Gessner 2001: 8495.

east Asia and Oceania. London and New York: Kegan Paul International, 15-56.

Benjaminsen, Tor A., Ian Bryceson, Faustin Magaya and Tonje Refseth (2011): Conservation and Land Grabbing in Tanzania. Paper presented at the International Conference on Global Land Grabbing, 6-8 April 2011, Institute of Development Studies, University of Sussex.

Bryde, Brun-Otto (1986): Die Rolle des Rechts im Entwicklungsprozess – Rechtsvergleichendes Generalreferat. In: Bryde, Brun-Otto and Friedrich Kübler (eds.): *Die Rolle des Rechts im Entwicklungsprozess. Referate der Fachgruppe 'Grundlagenforschung' anlässlich der Tagung für Rechtsvergleichung im September 1985*. Frankfurt/M.: Alfred Metzner Verlag, 9-36.

Burg, Elliot M. (1977): Law and Development: A Review of the Literature and a Critique of 'Scholars in Self-Estrangement'. *American Journal of Comparative Law* 25, 492-530.

Carty, Anthony (ed.) (1992): *Law and Development*. Aldershot: Dartmouth Publishing Company (The International Library of Essays in Law and Social Theory).

Davis, Kevin and Michael Trebilcock (2008): The Relationship between Law and Development: Optimists versus Skeptics. *American Journal of Comparative Law* 56, 895-946.

Faundez, Julio (ed.) (forthcoming 2012): *Law and Development*. 4 volumes, London: Routledge.

Galanter, Marc (1966): The Modernization of Law. In: Weiner, Myron (ed.): *Modernization. The Dynamics of Growth*. New York: Basic Books, 153-165.

Galanter, Marc and David Trubek (1974): Scholars in Self-Estrangement. *Wisconsin Law Review* 1974, 1062-1102.

Gastorn, Kennedy (2008): *The Impact of Tanzania's New Land Laws on the Customary Land Rights of Pastoralists: A Case Study of the Simanjiro and Bariadi Districts of Tanzania*. Wien and Berlin: LIT Verlag.

Gessner, Volkmar (2001): Law as an Instrument of Social Change. In: Smelser, Neil J. and Paul B. Baltes (eds.): *International Encyclopedia of the Social and Behavioural Sciences*. Amsterdam: Elsevier, 8492-8496.

Hatchard, John and Amanda Perry-Kessaris (eds.) (2003): *Law and Development: Facing Complexity in the 21st Century*. London: Routledge Cavendish.

Honey, Martha (2008): *Ecotourism and Sustainable Development: Who Owns Paradise?* 2nd ed. Washington DC: Island Press.

John, Anja (1998): Traditionelle Rechte als Entwicklungspotential – mit Bezügen zu afrikanischen Rechtsordnungen. In: Institut für Entwicklungsforschung und Entwicklungspolitik (ed.): *Rahmenbedingungen von Entwicklung – Festschrift zum achtzigsten Geburtstag von Willy Kraus*. Saarbrücken: Verlag für Entwicklungspolitik, 245-294.

Juma, Ibrahim, Harald Sippel and Ulrike Wanitzek (2004): Tanzania: Peri-Urban Land Insecurity in Dar es Salaam. In: Woodman, Gordon R., Ulrike Wanitzek and Harald Sippel (eds.): *Local Land Law and Globalization.* Münster: LIT Verlag, 215-332.

Land Symposium Report (2005): *Experiencing the 1999 Land Acts: Where Are We now? Lessons for Policy and Practise. Report on the Proceedings of the Symposium on Implementation of the 1999 Land Acts Held at Courtyard Hotel, Dar es Salaam, 1st and 2nd March 2005*. Organised by Oxfam Ireland, Trocaire and Concern Worldwide. Funded by Development Cooperation Ireland (DCI).

Manji, Ambreena (2005): Cause and Consequence in Law and Development. Review Article of: McAuslan, Patrick, 2003: Bringing the Law back. In: Essays in Land, Law and Development, Aldershot: Ashgate. *Journal of Modern African Studies* 43, 119-138.

McAuslan, Patrick (2003): Bringing the Law back. *Essays in Land, Law and Development*. Aldershot: Ashgate.

Merryman, John Henry (1977): Comparative Law and Social Change: On the Origins, Style, Decline and Revival of the Law and Development Movement. *American Journal of Comparative Law* 25, 457-491.

Nader, Laura (2006): Promise or Plunder? A Past and Future Look at Law and Development. *World Bank Legal Review. Law, Equity and Development* 2, 87-112.

Nelken, David and Johannes Feest (eds.) (2001): *Adapting Legal Cultures*. Oxford: Hart.

Nelson, Fred (2007): Community-based Tourism in Northern Tanzania: Increasing Opportunities, Escalating Conflicts, and an Uncertain Future. In: Wishitemi, Bob, Anna Spenceley and Harry Wels (eds.): *Culture and Community: Tourism Studies in Eastern and Southern Africa*. Amsterdam: Rozenberg, 105-121.

Pande, Rohini and Christopher Udry (2005): Institutions and Development: A View from below. Yale University, 5 November 2005. Available online: <http://www.econ.yale.edu/~cru2/pdf/institutions_draft.pdf>.

Seidman, Robert B. (1971/72). Law and Development: A General Model. *Law & Society Review* 6, 311-342.

Seidman, Ann, Robert B. Seidman and Thomas W. Wälde (eds.) (1999): *Making Development Work: Legislative Reform for Institutional Transformation and Good Governance*. The Hague etc.: Kluwer Law International.

Sen, Amartya (2006): What Is the Role of Legal and Judicial Reform in the Development Process? *World Bank Legal Review: Law, Equity and Development* 2, 33-49.

Sippel, Harald and Ulrike Wanitzek (2004): The Vitality of Local Land Law – a 'Fatal Vitality?' A Case Study of Peri-Urban Dar es Salaam, Tanzania. In: Probst, Peter and Gerd Spittler (eds.): *Between Resistance and Expansion. Explorations of Local Vitality in Africa*. Münster: LIT Verlag, 231-245.

Sulle, Emmanuel, Edward Lekaita and Fred Nelson (2011): From Promise to Performance? Wildlife Management Areas in Northern Tanzania. Available online: <http://www.tnrf.org/files/WMA_summary.pdf>

Tamanaha, Brian Z. (1995): The Lessons of Law-and-Development Studies. *American Journal of International Law* 89, 470-486.

Trench, Pippa Chenevix, Steven Kiruswa, Fred Nelson and Katherine Homewook (2009): Still 'People of Cattle'? Livelihoods, Diversification and Community Conservation in Longido District. In: Homewood, Katherine, Patti Kristjanson and Pippa Chenevix Trench (eds.): *Staying Maasai? Livelihoods, Conservation and Development in East Africa*. London: Springer, 212-255.

Trubek, David M. (2001): Law and Development. In: Smelser, Neil J. and Baltes, Paul B. (eds.): *International Encyclopedia of the Social and Behavioural Sciences*. Amsterdam: Elsevier, 8443-8446.

United Republic of Tanzania (1997): *National Land Policy*. Dar es Salaam: Ministry of Lands and Human Settlement Development.

Wanitzek, Ulrike (2005): Land Law and Legal Pluralism in Tanzania: Security of Customary Land Tenure? In: Rösel, Jakob and Trutz von Trotha (eds.): *The Reorganisation or the End of Constitutional Liberties? La réorganisation ou la fin de l'État de Droit?* Cologne: Köppe, 179-198.

Weilenmann, Markus (2005): Ist Projektrecht ein Erfüllungsgehilfe von Organisationen der Entwicklungshilfe? Eine Fallstudie aus Burundi. *Entwicklungsethnologie* 14, 129-148.

Beiträge zur Afrikaforschung

hrsg. vom Institut für Afrika-Studien der Universität Bayreuth

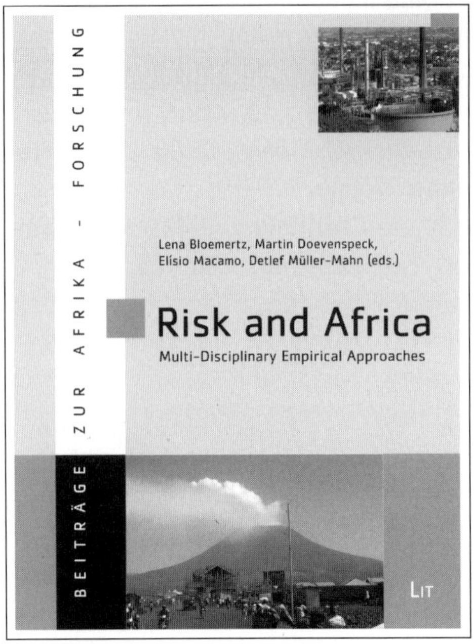

Lena Bloemertz; Martin Doevenspeck; El¡sio Macamo; Detlef Müller-Mahn (Eds.)
Risk and Africa
Multi-Disciplinary Empirical Approaches
Through a range of varied articles this book explores the changing nature of risk in contemporary African societies. It provides a valuable addition to current debate on the concept of risk which has traditionally been skewed in favour of European historical experience. The articles illustrate that technological hazards, pollution and climate change as well as the introduction of new forms of insurance and the restructuring of civil society are just some of the recent developments that invite us to be sceptical of prevailing notions of risk in the African context. The reader is encouraged to move away from focusing on the vulnerability of Africa as a pre-modern society to consider more localised and contemporary perspectives of risk.
Bd. 51, 2012, 288 S., 29,90 €, br.,
ISBN 978-3-643-90157-6

Gerd Spittler; Michael Bourdillon (Eds.)
African Children at Work
Working and Learning in Growing Up for Life
Most children in Africa start working from a very early age – helping the family or earning wages. Should this work be abolished, tolerated, or encouraged? Such questions are the subject of much debate: international and national organizations, employers, parents, and children often have diverse opinions and put pressure in different directions. The authors of this book contribute to the discussion through intensive fieldwork and careful analysis of children's activities. They consider childhood and family, work and play, work in rural and urban contexts, paths to learning, work and school, and children's rights.
Bd. 52, 2012, 360 S., 39,90 €, br.,
ISBN 978-3-643-90205-4